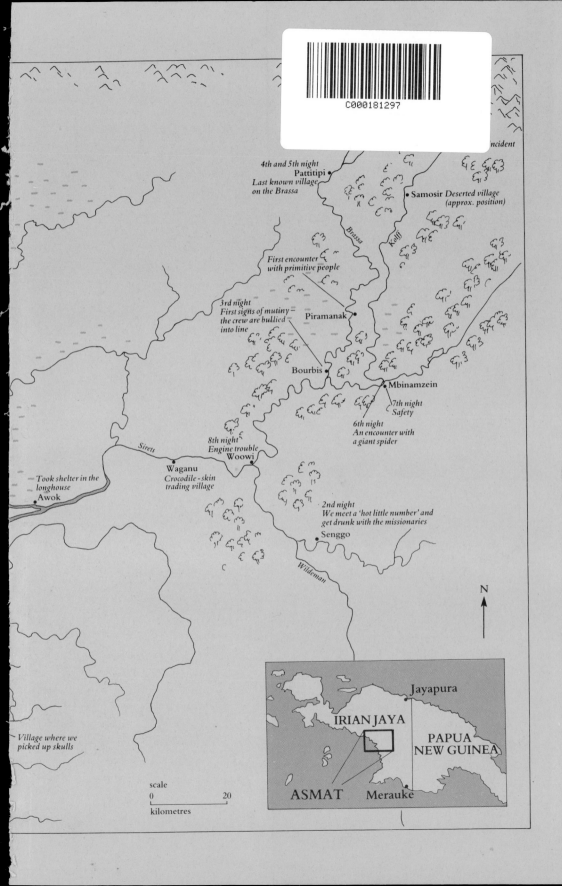

...ncident

4th and 5th night
Pattitipi •
*Last known village
on the Brassa*

• Samosir *Deserted village
(approx. position)*

Brassa

Kolff

*First encounter
with primitive people*

*3rd night
First signs of mutiny –
the crew are bullied
into line*

Piramanak •

Bourbis •

Mbinamzein •

*7th night
Safety*

*6th night
An encounter with
a giant spider*

Sirets

*8th night
Engine trouble*
Woowi •

Waganu •
*Crocodile-skin
trading village*

– *Took shelter in the
longhouse*
Awok •

*2nd night
We meet a 'hot little number' and
get drunk with the missionaries*
Senggo •

C

Wildeman

N
↑

– *Village where we
picked up skulls*

scale
0   20
kilometres

Jayapura •

IRIAN JAYA

PAPUA
NEW GUINEA

ASMAT   Merauke

SKULDUGGERY

SKULDUGGERY

Mark Shand and Don McCullin

JONATHAN CAPE
THIRTY-TWO BEDFORD SQUARE
LONDON

First published 1987
Copyright © 1987 by Mark Shand and Don McCullin

Jonathan Cape Ltd, 32 Bedford Square, London WC1B 3EL

British Library Cataloguing in Publication Data

Shand, Mark
Skulduggery.
1. Irian Jaya (Indonesia)——Description
and travel——1963-
I. Title   II. McCullin, Don
919.5'104   DU744

ISBN 0 224 02501 5

Typeset at The Spartan Press Ltd,
Lymington, Hants
Printed in Great Britain by
R. J. Acford Ltd, Chichester, Sussex

Contents

Illustrations

Photographs by Don McCullin, with the following exceptions:
nos 2, 3, 5, 7, 8, 9, 19, 21, 24, 27, 29, 42 and 44 by Mark Shand
and nos 4, 25 and 40 by Harry Fane.

For my father
M.S.

CHAPTER ONE

Relief Data Incomplete

The telephone rang as I was gazing aimlessly at the cold, wet view over St James's. I let the answering machine pick it up – I was trying to avoid almost everybody.

'Shand. McCullin here. Call me back if you ever finish lunch.'

I dialled his number in Somerset.

'Sorry Don. I thought you were the bank manager.'

'Now listen, Mark. You're getting soft and lazy. You need some excitement. How about organising another trip?'

'Where do you want to go?'

'Indonesia.'

'Again?'

'Why not? Besides,' he went on, 'I'm going mad down here. I'll scream if I see another cowpat. I need rivers, jungles and a few sunsets. Also, I've got a new pair of boots I want to try out.'

He was right. My stomach bulged over my trousers, my suntan had long faded and the dashing streaks of blond in my hair had turned to a sooty brown. It was time to get going.

★

I had first met Don in London in 1983. He was nursing a badly damaged arm, injured while covering the hostilities in San Salvador. In twenty years he had become one of the world's most distinguished and brilliant war photographers. Now he wanted to focus his camera elsewhere, on scenes as dramatic but without the tragedy. He also wanted to have some fun. During subsequent meetings we found we had the same sense of

humour, and an obsessive interest in jungle clothing. I had
suggested we should go to Indonesia, a country whose magic
had lured me back year after year.

Most people, when they hear of Indonesia, think of Bali – the
Pearl of the Orient, with its rituals and dances, its gentle
smiling people and its thousands of temples. But Bali is just one
jewel in a dazzling crown. Indonesia is the land of volcanoes,
vast unexplored rainforests, bustling cities, street markets,
mighty rivers and snow-capped peaks.

For over three centuries most of Indonesia was a Dutch
colony. In 1942 it was invaded by the Japanese and on 17
August, 1945 became an independent nation. The world's
largest archipelago, it is made up of 13,600 islands girding the
Equator to the north and west of Australia, across 3,000 miles of
tropical seas. If superimposed on a map of the Northern
Hemisphere, it would stretch from England to Afghanistan.
Considering only a few thousand of the islands are truly
populated, the potential for exploration is unlimited. It is here
you can find the world's largest flower (the Rafflesia), the
largest lizard (the fearsome Komodo Dragon), the largest
Buddhist monument (Borobudur) and the bird of paradise.

Parallel to the west coast of Sumatra runs a long chain of
islands whose central links are the Mentawai group. Although
only sixty miles from the mainland, they have been separated
from it by a deep oceanic trench for about half a million years,
giving the islanders a unique culture which has developed in
isolation.

In 1984 Don, his youngest son, Alexander, and I travelled by
bus from Jakarta to Padang, a city situated on the west coast of
Sumatra. Our destination from there was Siberut, the largest
and least populated of the Mentawai islands. Due to infrequent
sailing schedules, we were stuck in Padang for a week. In
desperation, we bribed the owner of a small fishing boat, who
didn't have a licence to carry passengers, and were obliged to
hide like illegal immigrants in the hot and stinking hold to avoid
detection by the harbour police. Our intention was to track

down a remote tribe who lived on the west coast of the island, but adverse weather conditions, the lack of a seaworthy boat, and vigilant and greedy officials forced us to adopt a new plan. We hitched a ride on a vessel going to Sarabua, a village further north on the east coast of the island. We based ourselves at the house of the hospitable local teacher. Using his canoe and under his guidance we managed to reach several primitive Mentawai settlements. On one occasion, having hacked our way through thick rainforest, we stumbled on a bizarre ceremony. One of the villagers was dying of malaria and was laid out in the communal longhouse. At intervals, announced by the beating of a wooden gong, the natives would circle his body, chanting and ringing bells. Their costumes were astonishing. They wore flamboyant head-dresses of flowers, feathers and palm leaves; their loin-cloths of bark from the bread-fruit tree were crimson, ensanguined with the juice of berries. Brightly coloured bands of glass beads encircled their arms and necks, and their torsos were tattooed with a series of lines that spread like spiders' webs down their bodies. Because of my own tattoos, the chief of the village considered me a brother. He even offered me a Mentawai version which I politely declined.

Later, a pig was killed and after the feast, a dance. Leaping to their feet, the men shed their finery and, half-naked, illuminated by the glow of the fire, were transformed into creatures of the jungle. Odd, slow bobbing movements portrayed birds drinking at the river, a graceful arm motion became a soaring eagle, culminating in a frenzied whirl as a python crushed its prey.

Before our departure, the chief presented me with the antlers of a buck he had shot. My gift, in comparison, seemed inadequate – an old passport photograph and a ten-pence piece. We returned to the mainland, legally this time, on board an old tramp steamer on which a market had been set up, offering everything from dried fish and mouse-deer to armadillos and aphrodisiacs. I watched Don wandering around taking photographs, totally immersed in the atmosphere, and as I took my

first gulp of beer in a month I realised that he, too, had been
captivated by the subtle charm of Indonesia.

★

'As you know, Don, Indonesia is rather large. Where do you
want to go?'

'Irian Jaya.'

'Why?'

'Well, I thought as we had reached the most western point of
the archipelago last year, why not now go to the farthest east,'
Don said. 'They still eat people there.'

'Oekaayy,' I said slowly. 'I'll do some research.'

We left it there and rang off.

I pulled out an atlas. Irian Jaya spread like a green and brown
slug across the page. Its size and emptiness were daunting.

Irian Jaya is the Indonesian or western half of New Guinea,
the second largest island in the world. The eastern half, Papua
New Guinea, once a British and German colony and then an
Australian protectorate, became an independent state in 1975.
Formerly Dutch New Guinea, Irian Jaya was relinquished to
Indonesia in 1963 after a short military campaign engineered by
President Sukarno. Although the region is potentially rich in
oil, timber and minerals, exploitation has been limited to
certain coastal areas. It is still largely unexplored: there are
tribes who have never seen a white person, cannibals and
headhunters whose lifestyle has remained unchanged for
thousands of years. It is one of the most remote and primitive
regions on earth.

I remembered a friend who had been there and contacted
her. Her journey had taken her to the Grand Baliem Valley in
the highlands of central Irian Jaya, which is inhabited by the
Dani tribes. This region, she told me, had already been well
trod and the natives, sporting their impressive penis-sheaths,
had become the subjects of picture postcards. These people
dried their dead, and charged money to foreign tourists who
wanted to take pictures of them. In fact, when the Dani learnt

of her arrival, they displayed the most recent corpses, decorating them with flowers and adorning their heads with plastic bags.

She had heard of another tribe who lived in the Asmat, a remote, crocodile-infested area on the south coast. Headhunting and cannibalism were still common among them, the people skilled craftsmen whose striking wood carvings had become collectors' items. It was there that the young anthropologist, Michael Rockefeller, had disappeared in the 1960s.

Headhunters, crocodiles and booty – it took about thirty seconds to sell the idea to my oldest friend, Harry Fane. We had both travelled extensively in Indonesia and about six years ago built a house in Bali. We had first gone there in 1973, lured by the fantasy of this mystical island. A friend had drawn a map on the back of a cigarette packet, directing us to a unique development that had fallen into financial difficulties and was now run by the local village. It was paradise. Beautifully constructed thatched houses were set among waving palm trees on a deserted beach. Each year we returned, living like kings in feudal isolation, exploring the island and falling deeper under its spell.

We arrived one year to find the development had been taken over by a large hotel chain. A telephone now sat ominously on the reception desk and a stranger with a smile showed us the room tariff. It was time to move on. We decided to build a house of our own. A suitable plot of land was found farther along the beach, designs were drawn up and a workforce installed. Unfortunately it did not stay long, due to a heap of bones exhumed when the foundations were being dug. It appeared that our house was being built on a lepers' graveyard.

In Bali, it is difficult to sneeze without a ceremony. The local priest was summoned. Holy water was splashed around, incantations were muttered and a suitable contribution offered before our land was proclaimed clean. Work recommenced and gradually, out of the jungle, Garuda Park appeared – octagonal in shape, the grass-thatched roof supported by pillars made from coconut trees, each room looking out on to a central garden. A sign at the gate reads, 'If you are a friend of a friend, go away.' It is the perfect retreat.

Over the years, we have journeyed throughout Indonesia, to Java, the Celebes and the Moluccas or Spice Islands. On one occasion we sailed, accompanied by another friend and two Balinese in a local outrigger canoe, along a group of sparsely populated islands running east of Bali, to Komodo. On this island lives the fierce Komodo Dragon, which can grow to over four yards in length. We staked out a goat as bait and photographed the dragons at the kill. When we tried to crawl closer their aggressiveness was confirmed; they rushed at us and only by bombarding them with rocks and then climbing up into the safety of a tree did we escape injury. Nowadays, viewing the dragons from the safety of an elevated hide has become a tourist attraction. On our return, the wind blew us off course and we drifted for five days, without seeing land, living on dried fish and avoiding the whales. A collision with one of these giants would have reduced us to matchwood.

We were, therefore, familiar with the country and its peoples, particularly Fane, whose mastery of the language was impressive, though we both doubted his knowledge would extend to the tribal areas. Don, though accustomed to perilous situations, had never before travelled in such dangerous areas without the back-up of a powerful communications machine. We were all unaware of what was in store for us – of course that was half the fun, the challenge of the unknown and therefore the impossibility of being prepared.

We now had to agree on a suitable date for departure. Fane and I are business partners – we buy and sell antique jewellery and objects made by Cartier – and we were approaching our busiest period. Don was booked to take photographs for the Guinness calendar in Kenya. We decided to meet at the Mandarin Hotel in Jakarta on 6 August.

Next, we compiled lists of essential items for our personal comfort. Before long, we were cruising round London's army surplus stores, stocking up on mosquito nets, hammocks and jungle fatigues. Whatever else, we were certainly going to look the part. Top of Don's list was food, as local cuisine does not agree with him. I remembered those mysterious silver packages during the previous year's trip, packages that rattled enticingly when shaken . . . and how pleased I had been to see them when we were dying of hunger. Fane and I were both prepared to eat local food, but agreed to contribute to the provisions by purchasing packets of dried soup.

I then paid a visit to my doctor. This was the high point of preparations as far as I was concerned. I am generally acknowledged to be one of the world's great hypochondriacs. I have a passion for pills, needles, bandages, ointments – anything connected with the medical profession. He put together a splendid jungle-survival kit which contained everything I might possibly need – including an anti-snakebite device, a whole assortment of dressings and a sharp and gleaming scalpel which I couldn't wait to test. I also learnt how to stitch wounds and give injections. My patient was an orange which was soon lacerated and punctured from my clumsy efforts.

During these days of organisation I wrote several letters to Indonesia, which I hoped would prove useful and perhaps smooth our way through the country's rigid officialdom. I had already met the British Ambassador to Indonesia and admired him greatly. I wrote telling him of our impending adventure, and received an enthusiastic reply promising us all the assistance the Embassy could offer. Also, I contacted my father's half-sister, Elspeth Howe, wife of our Foreign Secretary. I inquired whether messages might be sent via the Foreign Office to our Embassy in the part of the world to which we were going so that at least our identities might be known should we get into trouble. With her usual generosity she agreed to assist, and it was certainly no fault of hers that the initial signals were dispatched to Malaysia rather than Indonesia.

To assist us even further, I had a secret weapon, Deo J.

Hariandja. He had appeared in my life at a bus terminal in downtown Jakarta, a year ago when I was making inquiries about transport to Sumatra. The information was hopelessly muddling. Sweaty and frustrated, I had retired to the local police station where glasses of sweet tepid tea and prurient questions about the Princess of Wales preceded the theft of my cigarettes. There was a tap on my shoulder. I turned around; a small pompous figure, with a belly like a Buddha, was standing beside me, a briefcase clutched in his hand. Around his neck swung a bulky ancient Kodak, which I later discovered had no film. In broken English he offered his assistance. Within seconds my cigarettes had been returned, the Princess of Wales reclothed and the proper bus organised. I soon learned that my benefactor was a 24-year-old Batak, liked sex, music and adventure, and was a reporter for a small Jakarta magazine 'on assignment', when he noticed my distress. The Batak people come from an area surrounding the great inland lake of Toba, in northern Sumatra: they are loyal, fearless and fiendishly cunning. Deo was bored by his job, and I offered him the chance to explore his own country with us, in the capacity of guide and interpreter, slave and general dogsbody. Equally promptly he accepted. My instincts proved correct; Deo was invaluable on that first trip and Fane and Don agreed that he was our man.

I wrote letters to each of his six addresses, and one eventually reached him. He replied that he would be waiting at the Mandarin Hotel, to which I had introduced him the year before and where he had instantly acclimatised to room-service and air-conditioned splendour and spent many hours whizzing up and down in the elevators – to the irritation of the other hotel guests.

By the end of June, Fane and I felt we were ready. We had air tickets, passports, emergency food rations and a map of Irian Jaya. I even remembered to take my wireless as England would be playing Australia for the Ashes. A week later our valuable Cartier objects were locked away in the bank vaults. The alarm was switched on and we slammed the front door, leaving only the expensive scent of our last satisfied client lingering in an empty office. Fane flew direct to Bali, while I went to Hawaii for a few weeks. We met up in Garuda Park at the end of July.

★

The man who runs our house in Bali had contacted his cousin, a policeman called Mayorpol (Major) Wayan Diana, who had been stationed in one of the most remote outposts in Indonesia – Merauke, on the south coast of Irian Jaya. This was to be our stepping-stone to the Asmat region. Fane and I fired questions at the Major. Where would we find the most dangerous and primitive people? Which areas had never been penetrated by white travellers? He pointed to our map, indicating a spot north of the Asmat region. Peering over his shoulder we could read the words 'Relief Data Incomplete'.

Even with the aid of a magnifying glass we could barely decipher the names of the huge rivers we would have to navigate to reach this region: rivers with names such as Brassa, Kolff and Sirets. Fane and I listened intently. In this remote area lived the true people of the jungle, the 'orang hutan', nomads who were seldom seen, unpredictable and possibly extremely dangerous. According to local crocodile-hunters and police, the 'orang hutan' concealed themselves in the dense foliage on the river banks, attacking passing canoes with poison-tipped arrows. Fane and I exchanged glances – this was the destination we had dreamed of in London. The Major left us with a parting admonition to proceed with the utmost caution.

We packed our rucksacks and kitbags and boarded a flight to Jakarta to meet Don and the fat Batak.

CHAPTER TWO

Last Luxuries

Jakarta is the sort of city you either love or hate; it is dirty, aggressive and furiously busy, with a pulse I find irresistible. The atmosphere is a unique mixture of rain on hot slate roofs, human sweat, and the sweet sickly smell of rotting vegetation. Fiercely competitive taxi-drivers, all frustrated Fangios, weave their way through the congested streets defiantly ignoring all laws and obstacles. Soon we were speeding towards the hotel. The skill with which Fane, in swift and efficient Indonesian, had established the proper price for the journey stunned our driver into total silence. From time to time he would cast murderous glances into his mirror, only to find our faces stonily impassive as we stared past him through the windows. As it was early morning, the wooden latrines balanced precariously on the banks of the canals were jam-packed; occasionally I caught a fleeting glimpse of squatting figures, their faces screwed tight in concentration as they performed that most important of morning rituals. Leaving behind the shanty towns, we roared into the world of high-rises and there, like a monumental ice-cold vodka and tonic, dripping with condensation, stood the Mandarin Hotel.

We were welcomed by our friend Martin Reed, the Resident Manager, and by Don, who was not in a good mood. He had arrived two days earlier and was now impatient to get going. To make matters worse, Deo had appeared with a certain Mr Wim in tow who, the Batak had assured him, was the key to our expedition. Don was not convinced, as Mr Wim's only contribution so far had been to add to Don's bill by ordering vast quantities of food at the hotel coffee shop.

At the reception desk there was a letter waiting for me from Margaret Rothwell, Chargé d'Affaires at the British Embassy. Unfortunately, the Ambassador was away on home leave, but we were invited for lunch the next day.

We rose early, for we had only two days in which to organise everything before we caught the plane to Irian Jaya. Our first priority was to obtain a *Surat Jalan*. This is a letter from the police permitting the bearer to travel through the more remote areas of the country and *essential* for visitors to Irian Jaya. We knew an influential Indonesian, at whose offices we handed over our passports and photographs and a rough itinerary of places we wanted to visit. We were assured that everything would be in order the next day, an unlikely outcome without a friend in high places.

Back at the hotel, waiting for us in the lobby, clutching the inevitable sheaf of papers, was Deo. It was an emotional reunion; I was delighted to find him as fat and cunning as ever, and he was clearly relieved to see me, for he kept casting nervous glances at Don. Before long, though, Fane and he were jabbering away in Indonesian, Deo pouring scorn on my ineptitude in the language. When I left Jakarta the previous year, I had promised to bring him a gold necklace, which I now produced and duly hung around his fat neck. He seemed pleased, but nevertheless squinted down suspiciously and bit it. He was anxious to introduce us to Mr Wim, so we arranged to meet them at the coffee shop, later in the afternoon.

Having donned our best tropical kit, we crossed the square to the British Embassy. Security was rigid; our credentials were thoroughly checked. We were ushered along by a rather scruffy individual who had been toying with one of the receptionists when we arrived. Evidently he was in a high state of excitement, frantically trying to adjust his trousers as we went up in the lift.

Margaret Rothwell was courteous and helpful. After we had outlined our rather vague plans, she produced an impressive document, heavily embossed with a blue seal, listing us as

British subjects well known to the Embassy, and assuring the reader of our virtuous characters.

Lunch was served in the garden of her home, situated conveniently next door to the Embassy. We were joined by another guest, Mark Scrase-Dickens, who was the First Secretary or, in other words, the Political Officer. We all felt under some scrutiny, but he was an engaging companion: charming, amusing and a mine of information about Indonesia. When finally we left, it was with promises of good behaviour and of upholding the flag.

Our *Surat Jalan* had already been processed and was waiting for us at the hotel. Don disappeared to buy more film, while Fane and I headed to the coffee shop. Deo's friend Mr Wim was small, hairy and mysterious, and seemed more interested in the menu than in us. Between mouthfuls of chocolate cake, he promised letters of introduction to well-placed dignitaries in Irian Jaya. Somehow we doubted his importance, particularly when Deo whispered that I should pay his train fare home. We extracted ourselves as quickly and politely as possible.

★

Night-time Jakarta – a city that picks up tempo as the light fades. I suggested we check it out.

'If it's anything like the place you dragged me to last year,' Don said, 'I'm not coming. It took me a week to recover. I'm a respectable man. Meet you in the lobby in five minutes.'

Suitably fortified from the mini-bar, we entrusted ourselves to a taxi-driver. The streets were alive. The smell of satay and *kretek* (clove cigarettes) floated through the window. Hooting furiously, our driver squeezed past the food vendors. They pushed their little stalls unhurriedly, ringing a bell to attract customers. We swept into broader avenues. At an intersection a policeman, his uniform stained with sweat, blew a whistle ineffectively as the traffic roared around him. Above, advertising a brand of toothpaste, a young girl grinned down at us from a huge billboard.

We arrived at our destination and, when we paid our entrance fee, a young man with long, curling fingernails and an Afro hairdo stamped the back of our hands with a pink mark.

'This, in case you want to leave for a time,' he leered. 'When you come back, you no pay.'

We descended a dimly lit staircase, its worn purple carpet dotted with cigarette burns, into a large room that smelt of stale beer. Four immense speakers pumped out a pounding rhythm. A mirrored orb suspended from the ceiling revolved slowly, fragmenting the flashing lights that bounced off it. The room was almost empty. On the dance floor a few bored girls moved woodenly with each other.

'I think we're a little early,' I yelled. 'Let's get a drink. I'm sure it will hot up.'

Something tapped me on the bottom. I looked down on a mass of long, dark hair.

'American?'

'No, English.'

'Ah, no good. American better. American always much money. Goodbye.'

A few moments later a plump, taloned hand clutched at my sleeve. Her matronly features split into a sticky grin as I escorted her on to the now-crowded dance floor.

'You're lucky it's dark and you're blind drunk,' Fane yelled after me.

What the hell, I thought. I might as well enjoy myself. I began to gyrate and spin and jerk. The music flowed through my veins. I was feeling great. A slow number came on. Closing my eyes, I held out my arms to encircle the soft shape in front of me. For one moment I felt the cold hardness of a shirt stud against my nose, the next I was flat on my back. I peered up to see a huge, bearded man standing, glowering over me.

'Look, I'm frightfully sorry,' I said, stumbling to my feet and looking frantically for my dancing partner. 'You see, I thought you were . . .'

'Bloody oath! A bloody Pom too!' he snarled. 'If you weren't so bloody rat-arsed, I'd flatten you. Stick to your own kind, you bloody bum-bandit.'

I backed away hurriedly towards the bar where I found Don and Fane, convulsed with laughter.

'Jesus, what the hell are you laughing at? I nearly got killed. Let's get out of here.'

*

Having recovered from early-morning hangovers, we decided to visit the bird-market. A million birds and odd Indonesian animals are displayed in a huge covered area. The din and stench are overpowering. As we walked around, we were offered everything from glossy black cockatoos to lemurs – the sloth-like monkeys whose lives are spent hanging upside-down and eating. I caught the eye of a tufted eagle as it glared from under long eyelashes. Fane and I bought flight whistles for our homing pigeons in Bali. We left, covered in birdshit and almost deaf.

The Batak was waiting for us in the hotel lobby, holding a small bag in addition to his customary briefcase. He was packed and ready to go and had decided to move in with us for our last night in Jakarta.

In the afternoon we went our separate ways, checking our kitbags and rucksacks and stocking up on luxury items. The hotel was puzzled by our request for two dozen loo rolls and numerous bars of soap; several rather grand fluffy white towels were 'borrowed'. Our supply of empty vodka and gin bottles from the mini-bar was requisitioned and carefully filled with water. Don and I then paid a visit to a local department store to buy rope and (vital for keeping our kit dry) their entire stock of plastic garbage bags. I also needed a bed and eventually settled on a sickly green plastic sleeping mat, decorated in a colourful flowery print.

Mark Scrase-Dickens had invited us to dinner. Wary of leaving Deo alone to sample the delights of room-service, I carefully hid the menu, as I remembered his voracious appetite from the previous year. Leaving him with a pre-ordered meal of rice and eggs, we set off too excited and preoccupied to be in the mood for social chit-chat. We had expected our host to be married to some hard-working and worried helpmate suitable for a First Secretary in foreign parts, but Tina Scrase-Dickens turned out to be charming, voluptuous and amusing, a wonderful hostess whose image would no doubt grace our dreams during the next few weeks. The meal was a lighthearted affair served at a table gleaming with silver and initialled matchboxes, marred only by the *constant* appearance of young Scrase-Dickens, an extremely excitable boy over from England for the school holidays. His bombacity finally became too much and he ended up squealing for mercy as I dangled his head in the loo bowl and pulled the chain.

With drunken promises of exotic objects for Tina on our return, we stumbled back to the hotel to find Deo snoring and surrounded by piles of empty plates. He had found the room-service menu. Kicking his slumbering form, I threatened him with three days of starvation; he grunted, rolled over and went back to sleep. Don found a document lying by Deo's bag identifying the Batak as a reporter. He announced emphatically that unless it was left behind he would be quitting the expedition; in his experience, it was suicide to take press credentials into sensitive areas. I argued that Deo was not exactly foreign correspondent for *The Times* but my pleas fell on deaf ears. Fane and I failed to see the difficulty but, respecting Don's experience, I assured him in the end that I would confiscate the offending article. The deal struck, it seemed sensible to get some sleep, for in a few hours' time we had to catch an aeroplane to Irian Jaya.

Three bleary-eyed adventurers, kitted out in full combat fatigues, assembled in the deserted hotel lobby at 3 a.m. After wolfing down croissants and coffee, we paid our bills and I discreetly transferred Deo's press pass into one of the bags we were leaving behind. In contrast to our early-morning surliness, the Batak himself was annoyingly wide awake and talkative, in his brightly striped sports shirt and tight grey shorts. With a funny little straw hat perched on his head, he resembled a schoolboy going back for the Summer Term, rather than someone about to embark on a perilous journey into unknown territory. I entrusted all our travel documents to him, and gave strict instructions that we were not to be disturbed until our arrival in Irian Jaya.

At the airport a new X-ray machine, its lights flashing, silently consumed and then spat out the checked-in luggage. For the second time in the space of four hours Don freaked out; utterly helpless, he could only watch as his suitcase, containing his precious stock of film, disappeared into the machine. I pointed out the sign which read: FILM NOT AFFECTED BY X-RAY.

He was convinced that it would be ruined and, as far as he was concerned, that meant the end of his part in the expedition.

'These people,' he groaned, 'are like children with a new toy. They have the power on so high it'd burn a hole in your underpants.'

CHAPTER THREE

Dead End

The flight headed north-east, crossing a huge expanse of the archipelago, stopping at Ujung Pandang in the Celebes, Biak – an island off the north coast of Irian Jaya – and finally at Jayapura, its capital. My recollections of the journey are dim. In the background, I remember hearing a continuous buzz of conversation as Deo exerted his charm over two totally uninterested stewardesses, and at regular intervals the clatter of plastic as he attacked another food tray.

Even at 5 p.m. the heat bounced off the tarmac as we disembarked at Sentani Airport, located alongside the large lake from which it takes its name. We crossed to the cool arrival shed, where Deo flew into a whirl of activity, snapping orders at sleepy porters and efficiently gathering our baggage into neat piles. While he organised transport into the city, the rest of us were subjected to the curious scrutiny that we always attract in Indonesia. One official caused me to wonder whether we had not overdone the Rambo image, and I ventured to suggest to Fane that we might tone down our outfits. Fane would hear nothing of this, having suffered agonising and lengthy dress rehearsals in Jakarta.

We piled into the minibus that would take us to Jayapura and soon were bumping along a high, winding road, hemmed in by dense jungle on either side. As we descended, we were afforded a fine view of the bustling port nestling in the hollows of the hills that surround it, and of the blue Pacific, beyond.

We made straight for the airline office to inquire about planes leaving for Merauke in the south of Irian Jaya. We were in luck.

There was a flight scheduled to leave early in the morning, and we hastily booked seats. It was necessary now to visit the Chief of Police, in order to get our *Surat Jalan* 'chopped' (stamped).

Within seconds of pulling into the compound of the police barracks, our minibus was surrounded, and for the second time I began to doubt the wisdom of the Rambo apparel. Apart from the difference in skin colour, and the side-arms they wore strapped to their thighs, there was little to distinguish the policemen from ourselves.

A few awkward moments passed before Fane took control of the situation. In a dazzling display of Indonesian, he explained our precipitate arrival. We had soon all become close friends, and were sharing cigarettes and accepting cups of tea in the barracks, while somebody was sent to fetch the Chief of Police from his home. Half an hour later we were courteously ushered into the office of Captain Made Mustika. Fane was now in full flow, and it was obvious from the delighted expression on the Captain's face that it had been a long time since a foreigner had stood in his office speaking with such eloquence and precision. And if Fane's command of Indonesian placed us in a good light, our owning a house in Bali ensured a place for ever in the Captain's favour: he too was from Bali. Not only this, but he owned a house and land in Kuta, fairly near our own! Well, what a coincidence . . .

As the spirited conversation wore on, I began to wonder how long we would have to stay here. Glasses of ice-cold beer shimmered before my eyes, while Don fought a private battle against the mosquitoes which sniped at his ankles. Our gaze was fixed on the Captain's hand, which held the vital chop . . . with bated breath we watched as it hovered enticingly over our *Surat Jalan*, willing him to deliver the *coup de grâce*. Three times the hand descended, only to float up again as the Captain launched into yet another enthusiastic discussion with Fane. At last, with relief, we watched it baptise our virgin document, and we were on our way.

Deo, who had disappeared during our ordeal, returned with

the news that he had found us a hotel. He was accompanied by the Captain's Second-in-Command, who turned out to be his cousin. It was beginning to resemble a game of 'Happy Families'; before they could invite us home to tea, we fled, excusing ourselves on the grounds of exhaustion.

After the claustrophobic police headquarters, the hotel seemed like a palace. Our room was clean and inexpensive, and the food passable, yet I was unable to satisfy my craving for ice-cold beer, for the key to the fridge had been mislaid. Cunning and resourceful as ever, the Batak soon had it prised open with my Swiss army knife.

The medicine chest offered slight relief to an ear infection I was developing, and after a few nips of whisky from my hip flask we all collapsed into our beds, already half-asleep.

★

We travelled in silence to the airport, noticing an unusual flurry of police and army activity on the way. I dispatched Deo to ferret out the reason for this while we waited for our flight to be called. A few minutes later, he returned with some astounding news. Only a few days before, south of Jayapura, two Japanese soldiers had materialised, as mysteriously as spirits. It turned out that these men had been living deep in the jungle for the past forty years, unaware that the war was over, and had at last emerged in order to surrender to the enemy. The incident drove home to me just how remote and little known this part of the world could be.

From the air we could just make out the highest peaks of the mountain range that stretched like a jagged comb across Irian Jaya. During the descent, the reflection of the plane danced over the deceptively serene surfaces of broad rivers. Soon we would be thinking very differently about them as we battled our way up in search of the orang hutan tribes.

There was the usual confusion at Merauke airport. We had hardly stepped out of the aeroplane before a particularly persistent policeman was pushing forward through the sea of grinning black faces and frizzy heads to demand our papers. With a disarming smile and the lure of one of Harry's precious Camel cigarettes, Deo soon had him under control. Our orders were straightforward: processing and paperwork at the police barracks as soon as possible.

Merauke has an air of total finality about it. It is, in fact, the end of the line: unless you intend attempting an expedition such as ours, you really cannot go anywhere from here. Two hours by car due east would take us to the Papua New Guinea border, which is a restricted zone. It would be a long row due south before we arrived Down-Under. Slowly the truth dawned, that we had managed to take not only the longest but also the least practical route to our destination, Agats. Had we bothered to find out in Jayapura, we could have flown from the capital to Wamena, high in the central mountain ranges. From there we could have chartered or begged a ride on one of the missionary aeroplanes flying direct to Agats.

It took us three hours to get our *Surat Jalan* processed. We sat in a row on a bench outside one of the offices as our papers and passports were transferred from the hands of one faceless official to another. Opposite was the police cell, black against the searing glare of the compound. From the gloomy depths long black arms reached through the bars, as the inmates pathetically and continuously called to us for cigarettes. From somewhere in those dank confines emerged the endless mad drone of one prisoner; not even the threatening whack of the guard's cane against the iron bars could silence him. Our papers were returned. Miraculously they were all in order.

Although our immediate thought was to get out of Merauke, as quickly as possible, we also had to organise in advance our transport up the rivers. It had been suggested that we should try to locate a Mr Launchaung. The police offered to have a message sent to him, requesting him to meet us at our hotel. We were also told of a boat service to Agats, though no one seemed certain of its sailing itinerary.

The room rates of the Flora Hotel had convinced us that,

despite Deo's assurances to the contrary, we should settle for the less auspicious Hotel Asmat. In the lobby, three men were sprawled in front of a television set, their eyes glued to a soap-powder advertisement. A vase of plastic flowers standing on a deserted pool table completed the decor. The rooms were laid out like a barracks; we took one for the four of us. Bathing and bowel facilities were situated outside, and I made a mental note not to visit this area unless I wore wellington boots.

Don and Deo left to deal with the film and try to discover more information about ways of escaping from Merauke. Fane and I remained at the hotel for Mr Launchaung. We did not have long to wait. As he sidled in he appeared suitably piratical for an expedition such as ours. Gold teeth glittering, he explained apologetically about the enormous cost of petrol in this part of the world, and calculated we would need at least twelve 44-gallon drums. He added that the cost did *not* include the price of himself, a guide, two canoes, two boat operators and two outboard engines, and went on to name a total figure which was absurd. We settled down to hard negotiation.

Don and Deo returned with good and bad news. Don's film had managed to survive the X-ray machine but, on checking at the mission, he had been told that not a single mission aeroplane would be heading for Agats in the immediate future. The cost of a special charter from Jayapura was out of the question. The missionaries knew nothing of a boat going in our direction. We could, however, leave in exactly one week on a new scheduled air service operated by Merpati (an internal Indonesian airline) between Merauke and Agats. The inaugural flight had left that very morning while we were waiting for our *Surat Jalan* to be chopped. We had one whole week to wait in this dump.

I noticed the Batak eyeing Launchaung with obvious distaste and suspicion. Taking me aside, he whispered vehemently that this man was no good. I was irritated; how could he possibly know, considering he'd only just clapped eyes on the man? Deo squinted mysteriously at me and tapped his nose with his pencil.

'I can smell it, boss.'

He assured me that we could rely on him to find the right man. What the hell? We had so much time on our hands, we could build the bloody canoes ourselves. Telling Launchaung to piss off, Fane and I slumped into gloom, while Don decided to wander down to the port.

I was lying on my bed gazing at the wall, where a large gecko was stalking a spider, when our bedroom door was flung open, and there, framed in the doorway, stood Don, panting and gasping for breath.

'Get your arses moving!' he yelled. 'There's a boat leaving for Agats in three minutes!'

For a fraction of a second we were frozen; then the sound of the ship's hooter broke the spell and we were galvanised into action, cramming scattered clothes into rucksacks and rushing outside. While Deo commandeered a passing truck, we flung an assortment of rupiah notes at a baffled employee, tumbled on board and sped off to the port. Brandishing fistfuls of cash under our driver's nose, we implored him to go faster. The vehicle screeched to a halt outside the port gates. Yelling at Deo over our shoulders to bring the bags, the rest of us sprinted to the quayside – in time to see our boat gliding majestically out of the harbour, signalling its departure with a final taunting hoot. Speechless with rage, I grabbed a loo roll which had fallen out of my pocket, and hurled it at the mocking sound. This thrilled the crowd which had by now gathered round us. They exclaimed and applauded as the paper hurtled through the air, unfurling gracefully into the boat's bubbling wake.

Like mechanical dummies, we picked up our bags and trudged back to the hotel.

We had no option but to wait. Too exhausted to bother with a meal, we picked idly at a tin of processed cheese, washing it down with whisky. We then roused ourselves enough to make life more comfortable by setting up our mosquito nets. Don and I had accustomed ourselves to these intricate devices the previous year, so we managed to erect them with relative ease.

1 Fishing, Brassa River

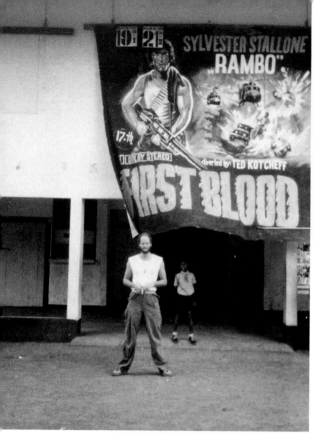

2 *Left*, the Honourable Harry
   St Clair Fane – Rambo, Blue
   Blood

4 *Opposite above*, Joseph in
   charge of the canoe

5 *Opposite below*, departure
   from Agats

3 *Below*, beauty and the beast –
   Jane Lummy and Don
   McCullin

7 *Above*, welcome? Warse village

6 *Left*, into the unknown

8 & 9 *Below*, Don and Deo, gourmets from different worlds

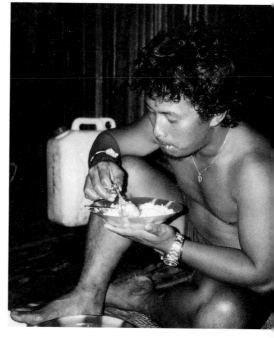

For Fane, however, this was a new challenge. On seeing his net spread out I regretted not checking the size when I bought it in London. The vast expanse of virgin cloth looked capable of covering the Great Bed of Ware. Enormous lengths of rope were required to hang it, and I made a mental note not to take a pee during the night for I was bound to garrotte myself in the process. Finally, it was up and Fane sank back gracefully, beneath its billowing canopy. His gauzy bed looked as cool and enticing as a bride's, and I laughed at the thought of him rigging it up in the jungle.

I lay awake in the dark, trying not to hear the rumbles of Deo snoring on the porch outside. He had been banished from the bedroom as Don found it impossible to sleep through his mighty crescendos. Sleep was eluding me too, and I started to calculate how many sleeping pills I could safely swallow to stay in a coma for the coming week . . .

Deo had already vanished by the time we awoke. No doubt he had discovered another Batak relation in Merauke. Contemplating another empty day stretching ahead, I forced myself to stay in bed. I considered writing a letter home, but on second thoughts couldn't be bothered. There was nothing to say.

The only answer seemed to be drink. I suggested strolling over to the more up-market Flora Hotel. The main street was deserted apart from small groups of youths lounging indolently on street corners; we could feel their eyes on our backs as we passed. A hot wind blew continually, slamming shutters loudly against the walls of silent houses. The coloured plastic bags which littered the street trapped the gusts of air and crackled eerily as they danced about. We were relieved to arrive at the hotel, whose lounge seemed positively welcoming after the street.

Sinking into rubbery velour chairs, we gazed vacantly at a greenish, half-empty fish tank and at several ethnic bows and arrows which hung desolately on the wall. In the background, live from Jakarta, Indonesia was playing football against Malaysia; the outside world suddenly seemed very remote. The beer was good at least, ice-cold and refreshing, and washed away the dust in our throats. We inquired whether there was a beach we might visit.

'Oh yes, sir,' the barman assured us, 'very beautiful, palm trees and white sand – only two kilometres that way.' He pointed at the fish tank.

An hour later, we reached this paradise. It was deserted, and there weren't many palm trees either. The white sand proved to be thick, cloying mud, which became even stickier as the weather changed: we were soon shivering chilled by the icy showers that lanced into our backs. A few splintered *prahus* (local fishing boats) lay abandoned, their wooden frames bleached bone-white, curved like the ribcages of some huge prehistoric creature. It was a thoroughly gloomy place and did nothing to raise our spirits. On the way back we passed a few children kicking a football around, and spent a humiliating half-hour attempting to match their skill.

Even the most remote bastions of the world can boast a Chinese restaurant, and Merauke was no exception. Between mouthfuls of searingly hot chili soup, we egged on a cat which had managed to drag a live rat twice its size from the kitchen and was toying spitefully with it. Suddenly, our attention was caught by a furtive whisper from the dark alley-way outside the restaurant. White teeth gleamed at us as he described his wares in impeccable English: 'Very cheap, very clean, very young!' Sadly, we declined; that was the last thing on our minds right then. Nevertheless, the episode was encouraging. It was the first hint of excitement that Merauke had revealed to us.

*

Fane and I went to the Merpati office at the airport the next day and confirmed four seats on the following Friday's flight to Agats. We took along our Garuda tickets so that we could also stop at their agents' and confirm the flights out of Merauke to Jakarta (via Jayapura) at the end of our trip on 7 September. On the way, I glanced idly over Don's ticket. It was invalid after 27

August! Before leaving London I had told him emphatically to buy the same ticket as ours, one with a timespan of six weeks in Indonesia. Quickly I checked the prices – sure enough, it was 200 dollars cheaper! We were now faced with a tricky decision: either we didn't mention this discrepancy until the time came to use it, or we told him and accepted the reaction we predicted. On our way back to the hotel we wrestled with our consciences, finally electing to tell him. It was a dumb mistake. Don denied all responsibility for the error, laying the blame entirely on the travel agent. Worse, just as we had envisaged, he refused to take the risk of using an invalid ticket, deaf to our pleas that it probably would not be noticed. He argued that he had planned to meet his girlfriend in Bangkok around the second week of September and didn't fancy being stranded in Merauke, clutching a useless ticket, an expired *Surat Jalan* and a 100-rupiah note. We were left with no option but to put aside some money from our already stretched budget to enable him to buy a new ticket. Fane and I feared that his behaviour would jeopardise our plans. The atmosphere was less than cordial.

While we had been juggling with tickets, Deo had discovered the perfect man for our expedition. A more complete contrast to Launchaung could hardly be imagined. Manu Lamera was softly spoken and plump, with the hands of a man more accustomed to paperwork than dragging canoes up rivers. His earnest, almost religious air and persuasive voice captured our attention. In a few choice sentences he proposed an attractive deal and then politely withdrew, leaving us to check our finances and discuss the situation. His figure, calculated by the day, would include two canoes and two outboards, the cost of petrol, two crew men, a guide and, possibly, an armed policeman to protect us. This last item convinced us that we were in business.

We had been advised to break down our money into small denominations. With the US dollar worth roughly 1,200 rupiah, and these coming in 100- and 500-rupiah notes (not to mention the coins), the total amount had filled a garbage bag when we had called upon the bank for exchange.

The room was blacked out against inquisitive eyes and we deposited the rustling contents on a bed. Fane took charge and, distributing three enormous piles of rupiah notes, ordered us to shut up and get counting. Before long all that could be heard was the muttering of large numbers and the dry shuffle of paper as thousands became millions. With aching fingers and dry mouth I had passed 1,330,403 rupiah, when a loud voice triumphantly announced:

'*Finished!* Three million, seven hundred and twenty-two thousand, one hundred and one rupiah, exactly.' And with a smug grin Don sank back on to his bed.

This was too much. I had completely lost track and flung down my bundle in disgust. It was some time before we reached an agreed figure. Next came the equally odious task of budgeting our trip accordingly.

The conclusion was that we could afford to go but for not as long as we had hoped. Unless we managed to reduce Manu's price we would have no surplus cash to buy food and trading articles – let alone fly out of Agats at the end of the expedition. In the event of an emergency, we would really be up shit creek. We dispatched Deo to find Manu and present our offer to him.

We scarcely had time to recover before a grim Batak returned. Manu Lamera had rejected our proposal and, worse, had informed Deo that a bunch of crocodile-hunters were extremely keen to hire his canoes. We therefore had to reach a decision promptly so that he could radio the mission in Agats to hold the boats for us. Clearly, beneath that pious exterior beat a heart of steel. The crafty bugger had us trapped. Back to our sums. By knocking one day off our trip we worked out that the money would just about cover our expenses. What the hell? We had travelled thousands of miles to one of the most remote places on earth and we were not going to give up now.

We instructed Deo to convey our acceptance to Manu and to invite him to meet us later in the afternoon to discuss details.

When he reappeared, Manu was accompanied by a young man. Piet was to be our guide. He had a quiet manner and the

Batak, I noticed, had taken an instant liking to him. Rarely does Deo form a favourable first impression of anybody, and I took this to be a good sign. Manu surprised us again by insisting that we should not pay him until our return; he merely required a down payment of 200,000 rupiah as a sign of good faith.

The light was fading; teacups were now filled with whisky. Drawing our chairs closer to Manu, we watched carefully as he traced our proposed route on the map and described what we might expect to find. To encounter the elusive orang hutan we would have to travel further up-river than any previous expedition had attempted to do, and there was still a 90 per cent chance we would be unlucky. Warfare was still common between the different groups and cannibalism widely practised. Almost certainly, they would never have seen white people before.

Producing a small piece of paper, Manu drew a weird design which represented a palm leaf cut into a strip and another one looped six times across it. If we found something similar strung across a track or entrance to a village, it meant that they were at war, and it would be judicious to leave as quickly as possible.

He advised us to move slowly and cautiously at all times, even when there was no obvious sign of danger. Then he told us that if we found evidence of tribal presence, we would have to tempt the people out by hanging tobacco in the trees. If we were patient, and lucky, they would probably overcome their fear and filter out of the jungle. Most important to remember, Manu told us, was not to show any distaste or revulsion when we came face to face: their body smell is totally repellant. We would also need material for bartering – everything from nylon fishing line, beads, T-shirts and mirrors, to axes, parangs and, of course, tobacco.

Before leaving, Manu added that within a few years these tribal people would almost certainly have vanished, for a multitude of reasons, one being the exploitation of the oil. It was incredible to think that even now, on the brink of extinction, they remained in a Stone-Age world, living exactly as they have done for thousands of years. Finally, Manu reminded us of Rockefeller's disappearance – and with that, he and Piet quietly said good night.

I dreamt I was playing cricket against the Indonesians, captained by a headless Rockefeller.

CHAPTER FOUR

Good Riddance

Each of us had now developed his own peculiar system to keep occupied and ward off Merauke blues. Don spent hours hunched over his bed, laboriously threading nylon fishing line through hundreds of brightly coloured glass beads which he had brought specially from England. Most important, as gifts to defuse a touchy situation, he had explained. Cross-legged, with his glasses perched on the end of his nose, he reminded me of an old gem dealer I had seen on a street corner in Bombay.

Fane had 'Rambo'. His wife had bought him this great knife for his personal protection, but as yet it had been limited to domestic use. Rambo's debut had been made on the evening when the Great Bed of Ware was under construction, slicing through rope with ease. Since then Don and I had been allowed a closer inspection. It consisted of one long and lethal blade, fashioned from Toledo steel and honed to exquisite sharpness. A hollow handle contained an emergency compass, waterproof matches, string, a needle and thread, and even a small but efficient first-aid kit. The whole implement could be transformed into a deadly catapult, and fitted snugly into a macho-looking green sheath which matched Fane's jungle fatigues to perfection. He spent hours each day oiling the gleaming blades and occasionally I would catch him checking the condition of his beard in its reflection.

As for me, I had caught a severe dose of packing fever. Hours would be spent reorganising my rucksack, but I never seemed to get it quite right. I kept packing and unpacking it, trying each time to decide whether I should put my medical kit at the bottom and cameras at the top, or vice-versa. By now this particular problem had become an obsession. The others seemed to accept it as normal behaviour, smiling and offering words of encouragement as I burrowed like a maddened ant.

We had run out of booze. Although Deo assured Fane and me that we would be able to find some in Agats, we thought it wise to replenish our stocks now, in case of emergency. Scouring the town proved fruitless until we followed our noses to a dark little store run by a wizened old Chinaman. He produced two bottles. Brushing away the clinging mesh of dust and cobwebs, I could just decipher the words 'French Brandy' and 'Valiant Whiskey' on the rotting labels.

On our return, we noticed that *Rambo, First Blood* was playing at the local cinema. Fane was delighted. I took a photograph of him looking suitably tough posing against the gory poster.

On the morning of our fifth day in Merauke Fane found that his plastic washing bag had been stolen during the night. He had hung it up to dry outside the back entrance to our room. He summoned Deo, explained the situation and threatened hideous revenge unless the missing washbag was returned within the hour. Deo took to his new role as private investigator with relish. Very soon, he had the hotel staff lined up and quivering with fear as he interrogated each one thoroughly – to no avail. No doubt the washbag would take on a new lease of life as an example of contemporary headgear at the 'Merdeka Parade'.

Meanwhile, Piet the guide had dropped by to remind us that it was the dry season in the Asmat area: the further up-river we travelled, the shallower the waters were likely to become. He suggested that we might find ourselves obliged to leave the canoes and continue on foot. I glanced at Fane, who was grimacing with distaste: he was not partial to exercise. With Piet's help, we drew up a list of all our supply needs and dispatched the Batak for a day's shopping. Piet joined him. They seemed inseparable already.

Merauke had been transformed overnight, and was alive with

activity as everyone prepared for *Hari Merdeka*, which takes place all over the country on 17 August. The celebration of the independence of Indonesia was to be a splendid occasion this year as it was the country's fortieth anniversary. Carpenters were busily erecting huge wooden portals which would span the streets; others hammered away at platforms for local VIPs. During the rehearsals for the marches, we passed the time leering at the young, giggling Girl Guides as they paraded past, hopelessly out of step. The streets were lined with flags, and in the distance we could hear the discordant trumpeting of band practices. Invigorated by the carnival atmosphere, Don and I were moved to take a walk. Fane, eyes glued to the suggestive sway of a pair of young buttocks, declined.

The sun shone for the first time in days, and both Don and I felt relaxed and organised. Wandering through a village, we passed swamps, blazing with purple water lilies; a startled kingfisher flashed an iridescent blue. A smiling man astride a tiny horse galloped by, his feet almost touching the ground, his saddle piled with saws and planes.

It was dark by the time we arrived back. There was no sign of Deo. We whiled away the evening, serenaded by the band practice and Don's tales of Saigon and Cambodia.

Next morning, in anticipation of leaving Merauke, Deo appeared like Father Christmas, staggering under the weight of a huge pile of boxes. Within seconds we had ripped them open and were fingering razor-sharp axes and sifting through mountains of rice. Rapidly the room began to resemble a bazaar: hideously coloured T-shirts and shorts were strewn around, but the scene was dominated by three 10-kilo cartons containing our tobacco. Opening one up, we gazed at the rows of fat, sausage-like slabs which nestled inside; the pungent aroma soon hung heavily in the air.

Outside in the street, another Merdeka march practice was in full swing. Spotting the enticing buttocks of the day before, Fane shot over to the window and invited their owner to join us. She was cute, flirted shamelessly and spoke perfect English.

Her name was Jane Lummy. We spent a pleasant hour trying to catch a glimpse of her knickers.

Our lechery was disturbed by the arrival of Piet in a state of agitation. He had come straight from the Merpati office at the airport, where they had calmly informed him that the pilot due to fly us out to Agats was lying sick in the Flora Hotel, grounded for three days. As if that wasn't enough, Merpati had for some obscure reason decided that when the pilot was sufficiently recovered, the aeroplane was to be flown straight back to Biak, ignoring Agats altogether. Deo had disappeared at the wrong moment. Flagging down the first car, we ordered the bewildered driver to take us to the Flora Hotel. We were prepared to bribe the pilot if necessary.

Our hammering at his bedroom door brought out a rather surprised middle-aged man, hastily tying his sarong. To our unsympathetic eyes he looked hardly ill at all, just a little haggard and red-nosed. His eyes widened noticeably when the honey-tongued Fane launched into a smooth and urgent description of our predicament and, like a magician, extracted a fat wad of notes. The pilot's eyes flashed back and forth between the tempting bundle and the knot in his sarong – but, in the end, allegiance to the company triumphed over more mercenary considerations. He explained that the risk to his passengers would be too great. More likely it was the risk of his own dismissal that worried him.

Next we threw ourselves on the mercy of the elderly Dutch missionary stationed in Merauke. Having been warned that missionaries are generally unhelpful, we were pleasantly surprised by this emaciated, gently spoken man who had dedicated the past thirty years to serving the Good Lord in this dump. He was also an artist, and proudly showed us the paintings hanging on the walls of his dwelling. His choice of subjects was wideranging; a large unfinished canvas of the Last Supper was flanked by small oils of nubile young girls with bare breasts. He offered us warm beer and listened sympathetically as we poured out our troubles. For a brief moment our hearts lifted when he mentioned that a Cessna which belonged to the mission was due to stop in Merauke on its way to Agats to collect two sick missionaries. The father thought it possible that we might be able to charter this aeroplane for around 800 dollars. We were beyond caring about such details. However, a single-engine Cessna can only carry a maximum of 370 kilos, excluding the pilot; swift calculations brought the total weight of the three of us, plus Deo and Piet, luggage, and 100 drums of mixing oil for the outboards to at least 500 kilos. It was impossible.

We thanked the missionary for his hospitality and left. The unfortunate Deo was awaiting us in our room, and all our frustration was taken out on him. Wisely he left.

We sat around drinking. It was hopeless: we were well and truly stuck and there were no guarantees that the same thing might not happen to the next week's flight.

Suddenly the Batak burst in at the door, and in one long rush poured out his breathless tale.

'I go see my highly important friend in Merauke, who Wim gave me a letter for – he's Batak like me – and he tell me he help us. We go quick to see Boss of Merpati at airport. Boss Merpati very frightened of my friend and we tell him if my English friends not go to Agats, maybe Boss lose his job as my English friends are near Queen and Prime Minister of England. Then I show him letter from Embassy. Boss immediately contact Big Boss Merpati in Biak and explain problem. Big Boss also very frightened and send down new pilot today and he takes us to Agats in morning.'

We sat stunned. The cunning little bugger had pulled it off, thanks to his mysterious friend and the now 'exalted' Wim. I slid a glass of whisky over. He raised it and with a sly grin returned our letter from the Embassy.

★

Heralded by a triumphant fanfare from the band, the Merdeka Parade was unfolding before us like a giant multi-coloured ribbon. We could almost imagine that Merauke was paying us a tribute: having survived the town at its most drab and devious, we were being honoured with a rare glimpse of its better side. Hundreds of pretty young girls, dressed in every national and traditional costume in Indonesia, danced flirtatiously by. Representing the Asmat region were fierce-looking warriors, their faces and bodies brightly daubed with paint. Brandishing spears and shields, they leapt high in the air, uttering blood-curdling war chants. Teams of young boys representing different sports caused havoc, as shuttlecocks from the badminton section flew up to become entangled in the overhanging palm trees, and the over-zealous soccer team directed their footballs at the swaying backsides in front. It was an extraordinary event. Every aspect of life in Indonesia was represented. There was even a birth-control float, an old truck filled with nuns.

With a roar of engines and clouds of diesel fumes, the parade culminated in an impressive display of military and naval muscle, including tanks and camouflaged armoured cars bristling with menacing machine guns. The naval section was not *quite* so well represented: a giant wooden mock-up of a submarine rumbled past, the conning tower stuffed with bewildered men in wetsuits and snorkels.

Throughout this affair we were constantly reminded of police presence. Blowing their infuriating whistles, they bullied and pushed around people who were simply celebrating, with passion and pride, the independence of their great country. One unfortunate member of the Asmat warrior troupe was even subjected to a severe beating. He had been executing an astonishing dance, obviously slightly intoxicated but by no means obnoxious. I last caught sight of him, now a pathetic and lonely figure stripped of his finery, desperately protecting his woolly head from police canes. We all knew where he would be spending the night.

The parade finished as abruptly as it had begun and the street magically reverted to its normal dreary state. The only proof that the spectacle had taken place were a few bright balloons caught in the trees.

CHAPTER FIVE

Missionary Positions

The tiny waving figure of Jane Lummy was enveloped in a plume of dust as we sped off towards the airport next morning. Moments earlier she had appeared, sweating and breathless, to see us off.

'*Selamat jalan*,' (goodbye) she shouted, running alongside the minibus as it moved off. 'My mother would like to meet you next time you're here . . .' Fat chance, we thought. 'And don't forget the knickers and roller-skates you promised to send me . . . !

At the airport we unloaded our provisions, and carried them on to the tarmac. On checking the baggage, I noticed that two or three of the large plastic jerry cans containing our engine oil were already leaking, and dark stains were spreading over one of the sacks of rice. We were surprised to be joined by some extra passengers whom Merpati had decided to put on our flight – a bizarre collection of blousy, bald-headed women who were vainly attempting to keep under control their squealing children, their chickens and a large pig. However, we all managed to squeeze on board and, with a warning from Don not to smoke (he too had noticed the leaking oil), we shuddered into the air.

Squashed into my tiny seat, I peered awkwardly out of the window and saw the town shrinking below us. I allowed my mind to wander over the nightmare of the last ten days, days which had raised our hopes only to deflate them with gleeful malice. Now it was behind us and I hoped I would never again set eyes on that godforsaken place. We were finally, if cumbersomely, on our way to Agats.

I gazed across the aisle at Deo, who was already snoring peacefully. If it hadn't been for this grinning Mr Fixit, we could well have spent weeks rotting in Merauke. Craning my neck, I glanced round at Piet, catching a glimpse of his dazzling smile and a thumbs-up sign. In no respect did he conform to the Irianese stereotype. He was delicately made, his finely chiselled features and ruddy complexion resembling that of a Peruvian Indian, though in fact he was a native of Flores, one of the chain of islands that run east of Bali. Piet had come to Irian Jaya ten years before and spent a great deal of time in the Merauke/Asmat area, working in the timber camps up-river, deep in the jungle. He was dressed in an extremely odd fashion for someone about to embark on this type of expedition. He wore thick black tracksuit bottoms, two red jerseys and a multi-coloured woolly hat reminiscent of Brixton. Considering the extremely high temperatures we would be experiencing, I thought it a curious choice of outfit.

There was a sudden lurch as the aeroplane hit an air pocket. The flashing sign, which read 'o smokin', signalled that we had begun the descent to Ewer, the airstrip which serves Agats. I peered out of the window again. Through a haze of dark clouds and lashing rain, a small bright green patch of land the size and shape of a village cricket patch was suddenly illuminated by a flash of lightning. Deo seemed uninterested when I kicked him out of his peaceful slumber. I, too, closed my eyes, but not to sleep: a natural coward when it comes to flying, I recalled that the last plane to land here almost skidded into the river at the far end of the strip.

Suddenly, with a roar of rage, Don shot out of his seat, causing the aeroplane to lurch dangerously. Held gingerly between his fingertips were his socks and boots, dripping and emitting a particularly pungent smell. Fane and I tried to stifle our laughter as we realised what had happened. Sitting in front of him were two children, who, terrified out of their wits, had both relieved themselves over his feet.

All things considered, our pilot executed a perfect landing.

Soon we were bumping and sliding from one side of the grass strip to the other. We had arrived.

As we left the aircraft and began unloading our luggage, a strangely quiet crowd moved forward to surround us. Hideous old women, their ears pierced by safety pins like primitive punk rockers, stared at us wordlessly; old men with rheumy eyes and running noses watched, fascinated, as each piece of luggage joined the pile in the mud. A whisper of excitement swept through the crowd when they spotted the boxes containing our tobacco. Both sexes were wearing tatty old T-shirts, and I hoped that this symbol of civilisation did not become too familiar a sight up-river.

We were to be accompanied on the boat to Agats by a surly policeman with an unhelpful face. He would not have looked out of place on a commando parade-ground. His camouflage fatigues were immaculate, the creases in his trousers so sharp and stiffly starched that I suspected he might have difficulty sitting down. Around his waist he wore a highly polished black belt, attached to which was a low-slung holster. I was surprised to notice it was empty. He also carried an impressive two-way radio, from which sprouted a ridiculously long aerial.

Bidding farewell to our intrepid pilot, we piled into the battered old motorboat which was awaiting us. Piet and Deo had gone on ahead, making precarious progress in a slim canoe powered by an outboard, so weighed down by our provisions that it sank almost below the water-line. Our own journey began rather well, and we were soon whipping up-river, dark mangrove swamps flashing past on either side . . . It was too good to last. Four times we abruptly ground to a halt, and by the time the boatmen had tinkered around with the engine, the current had swept us back several hundred yards. To make matters worse, it had started to rain. In my best Indonesian I politely asked our policeman why he didn't radio Agats to send out another boat. My request was greeted with stony silence. He continued staring straight ahead, occasionally shaking drops of rain from his woolly hair. Impatiently I grabbed the radio and, switching it on, fiddled with the knobs. Nothing happened. I opened the back and saw that it contained no batteries. In disgust, I tossed it back to him.

Several hours later, frozen and soaking wet, we limped into Agats. Leaving Deo to round up some strong Asmatters to carry our luggage, Fane, Don and I set off to find the residence of Manu Lamera, which he had kindly put at our disposal. The house was occupied by his nephew and family, but they courteously moved out of their sleeping quarters to accommodate us. The room contained one bed, which was allotted to Don, the most senior member of our party. Fane and I eventually managed to assemble our mosquito nets and bedding in the remainder of the limited space. Considering the state of the outside latrine, I was relieved to see a wooden shutter instead of a window. It enabled one to pee freely and in comfort, despite its looking out on to the Cathedral.

Deo brought us unwelcome news. Firstly, our charming policeman was asking the equivalent of seventy US dollars for the passage to Agats. Secondly, the Chief of Police was not only insisting that we take *two* policemen up-river for protection, but also wanted us to leave our passports and *Surat Jalan* with him in Agats. The ability of these people constantly to think up ways in which to relieve you of your money passes belief. It was high time for them to realise they were not dealing with dumb tourists.

Armed with our British Embassy document and instructed to discover the normal fare from Ewer to Agats, Deo was dispatched to tell the Chief of Police that we refused to take a second policeman, and to explain that Englishmen would rather die than give up their passports. If Deo needed a last resort, he could allow them a copy of our *Surat Jalan*. Still seething with anger, I noticed a fat man, wearing long white socks and a bright flowery shirt, lumbering innocently along outside. Needing an outlet for my aggression, I made him the target.

'Hey, you! Fatso!' I yelled. 'Lose some weight, you slob, or we'll have to fish you out of the swamp.'

Before long a note arrived from Deo.

The note from Deo

He had taken to calling me '*Harimau*' (tiger), presumably because of my fair hair and foul temper. As our problems with the police appeared to have been solved, we decided to wander around Agats.

★

Agats (or 'Mud City') holds little charm. The core of the town is a rectangular wooden walkway half a mile in circumference, built on rickety stilts and in various stages of decay. The stores and houses lead off from this, connected by thin slippery planks. It was extremely rash to attempt to walk and look around at the same time; one small error of judgment could cause one to crash through the rotten wood and land in an undignified heap in the putrid slime below. The town possessed two redeeming features: one was the Cathedral, the other the mission.

The Cathedral was a splendid building constructed out of corrugated iron and timber, and so dignified that it stood completely out of context in its surroundings. I arrived there hoping to have an audience with His Lordship, Bishop Alphonse Sowada, Bishop of Agats, only to be informed by a helpful black sister in a smart blue habit that the Bishop was in Rome, in audience with the Pope. The sister proudly told me that the Cathedral could hold a congregation of 1,000, and that 75 per cent of the local population had been converted to Catholicism. During the Sunday service it was usually filled to capacity, the unlucky few who failed to find seats praising the Lord in their Sunday best outside.

Accepting the sister's invitation, I stepped inside to a cool and airy interior of almost art deco design. At one end an imposing Black Madonna surveyed her domain.

Next door to the Cathedral stood the Catholic mission. It is run by Americans belonging to an organisation called the Crosier Mission, whose headquarters are in Minneapolis. The building was long and low, with a large cross prominently displayed on the outside. A young boy ushered us into a clean, quiet compound. The moment we stepped inside, I felt the overwhelming urge to shatter that pious and peaceful atmosphere. It was the same sensation one experiences in public libraries and dentists' waiting-rooms. The wooden floors were the colour of honey and highly polished. From the verandah, we emerged into a luscious, cultivated garden filled with flowering shrubs, orchids, fruit and vegetables. Clearly, my ideas of missionaries living in dangerous headhunting areas needed to be radically revised – a suspicion that was confirmed when we were introduced to the brothers on duty at the mission that day.

Brother Ed was most hospitable and charming. In honour of our distinguished company, he skipped off to change, returning a short while later showered, dressed in clean clothes, bringing with him a subtle fragrance of cologne. A large figure, attired in a fetching combination of singlet and shorts, was scrabbling around in an ice-box. Clutching three cans of Swan lager, he turned around.

'Hi! I'm Brother Jim. Have a beer.'

I stared at him in horror, for Brother Jim and the fat man I had yelled at earlier were one and the same. Realising my embarrassment, Don and Fane tactfully engaged him in conversation. He gave no sign that he had heard my abuse, launching immediately into an enthusiastic description of the mission's work. Throughout the conversation I remained silent, knowing that I might have jeopardised our chances of reaching an acceptable arrangement with the missionaries. Due to our present financial position, we wanted to pay half the cost of the charter in Agats and the remainder in Jakarta. As most senior and respected member of our expedition, Don undertook to broach this sensitive subject. Brothers Ed and Jim could not have been more helpful, agreeing to all our demands and promising to arrange for one of their mission Cessnas to be in Agats in September to take us out. They warned us, however, that due to the unpredictable weather in the area, we could expect to be stranded there for an indefinite period. An image of the three of us helping with the collection in the Cathedral flashed through my mind.

Steered on to the subject of our trip, the brothers were willing to answer our questions but were equally fond of embellishing their replies with long, rather dull stories. Though clearly avoiding the particular case of Michael Rockefeller, they were even prepared to discuss cannibalism in general. Innocently I asked them when the last case had been committed; they replied, 'probably yesterday'. How did they rate our chances of making contact with the orang hutan? From their own experience they guessed we would see nothing at all, although it was to be admitted neither of the brothers had ever ventured as far up-river as we intended to go.

Grateful for their help, we thanked them and arranged to return the next day to finalise details.

That evening Deo was in the doghouse. There was not a drop of whisky to be found in Agats. This was going to be a very dry expedition. Our only hope now was that we might come across an inebriated old missionary up-river. Serenaded by the snores rising from McCullin's large and comfortable bed, Fane and I lay awake, discussing the gloomy situation, finally concluding that we might well have to wait until our return to Jakarta for our next drink.

We were surprised to find Brother Jim, in a glamorous Hawaiian shirt, kneading dough, when we returned to the mission next morning. He offered us a plate heaped with the doughnuts he had already made. While we were still stuffing our faces another, younger missionary appeared, floating ethereally over the gleaming floor towards us. I caught Don's eye. Desperately trying to swallow my mouthful of sticky dough without exploding it like grapeshot, I gingerly shook hands with young Brother Virgil, who greeted us with a quavering 'salaam'.

We finalised our departure plans with Brother Jim, wincing at the sound of travellers' cheques being ripped from their stubs. Then, bidding him farewell, we left him to his baking.

There was a small museum in Agats which we thought deserved a brief visit to study the artefacts on display and form a clearer impression of what to look for up-country. Fane and I were already imagining Duke Street, St James's, crammed with strange and beautiful carvings. By far the most interesting exhibit was a collection of heads decorated with cockatoo feathers and beads. The temple of most of these skulls was disfigured by a large hole, made by a stone axe. The brain of the victim, which is believed to give special strength, is sucked out and eaten by the men. Now we knew what to look for.

Piet was waiting for us at Manu's house. Sitting quietly outside were three locals who greeted us with friendly grunts. So, this was our crew. We studied each one carefully, and introductions were made.

Our canoe driver was called Yoseb Manupura (Joseph). He obviously fancied his chances with the ladies – though personally I did not envy his role of gallant among the females of Agats. He was about thirty and powerfully built, with an irregular Zapata-type moustache crowning a broad smile. It seemed he was the most experienced of the crew, having travelled up and down the rivers frequently over the past few years. I liked him immediately, though Don and Fane eyed him with suspicion.

The driver of the supply canoe was a quiet, religious man called Marwoto – or Alphonse. He had a squeaky voice and was smaller than Joseph, though wiry and very strong. Our 'personal policeman' was Monce Arrongear, but we were to call him Pak Polici. A strange, thin individual, he dressed immaculately in a denim jacket and khaki trousers as perfectly creased as those of the policeman who had accompanied us from Ewer. He carried proudly a rusty old Mauser rifle and a Swiss army knife, to which he had attached an extremely pornographic keyring, depicting several fat blondes contorted into enterprising positions.

We trooped down the walkway to the port to be shown our canoes. I suspect we were all hoping for something less starkly functional, but we were assured by Piet, Joseph and Alphonse that these were the most superior canoes in Agats. Alongside them lay another which looked far more attractive, with a jolly awning covering most of its length. Not only was it more inviting than ours but also more practical, particularly in view of the fact that it rained more heavily here than in any other part of the world. Joseph was horrified by the comparison, stressing that an awning would reduce our speed and impede our progress through those parts of the river which are densely overhung with foliage. I was on the verge of pointing out that the awning could be removed if necessary when I realised the futility of further argument. These were our canoes and we would have to make the best of them. Unpainted and well worn as they were, they looked strong enough.

The larger of the two was about thirty feet in length, three-and-a-half feet deep and four-and-a-half feet wide. It had been hewn from a single tree, and the sides built up, presumably to protect the passengers and their goods from the spray. I pointed out several large holes in the for'ard end, but was assured that these would be filled with mud before our departure. Fixed at the stern was a battered 40-horsepower Yamaha outboard engine.

As Fane, Don and I were to travel in this craft, we spent some time working out the most economical way of storing all our equipment. Under the lip at the front we would keep the cooking utensils, the food and the lamp. Behind these would be stretched a roomy orange tarpaulin, under which we would stow all our personal belongings – cameras, mosquito nets, Lilos and trading goods. Directly behind the tarpaulin was space for Fane, Don and myself, balancing one after the other on tin boxes, then the two massive 44-gallon petrol drums we were obliged to carry with us. We had arranged via the mission radio to collect more fuel up-river at Senggo. Piet would sit on the fuel drums, and finally, at the controls, would be Joseph.

The supply canoe was smaller, only twenty feet long, and powered by a 15-horsepower outboard. As well as Alphonse,

Deo and Pak Polici, it would carry our food, oil, two more petrol drums and eventually all the booty we hoped to acquire *en route*, and most important, my sleeping mat, wrapped securely in two garbage bags. I had entrusted this to the care of the Batak, and if he let it get wet . . .

We could not expect a comfortable trip. I could foresee that any infringement of personal space in the canoes might well end in bloodshed.

CHAPTER SIX

Jungle Johnnies

Piet helped while away our last night in Agats with stories of Michael Rockefeller's disappearance. He was reluctant to talk about it at first, but soon opened up after a little Indonesian pressure from Fane. Apparently, Rockefeller was in a canoe with a local boatman when it overturned in the open sea, near Ochenep. Afraid of the sea, the boatman stayed with the canoe, while Rockefeller chose to swim for the shore. Some people maintained that he drowned, but according to the local people, he was eaten in revenge after a Dutch patrol had been forced to kill a bunch of troublesome Asmatters in a nearby village. Piet considered it more likely, however, that Rockefeller was washed ashore already dead, or barely conscious, to be discovered later by villagers who deemed it a waste of good food. The skull, it seems, is still hidden away, although fortunes have been offered for it.

Whatever the true story it was a sobering tale, and we all wondered how we might recognise Rockefeller's skull if the opportunity should arise . . .

A thunderous roar of rain on the corrugated roof announced departure day. We dismissed Piet's suggestion that we might postpone leaving until the rain stopped, and dressed suitably for the occasion in the T-shirts that Fane had had made for us in Bali. Written in bold black and red letters across the front were the words 'WARNING! CONTENTS NOT FIT FOR HUMAN CONSUMPTION' and on the back, 'IRIAN JAYA '85'.

Last-minute nerves and too many people gathering outside the Cathedral forced me to use the dreaded outside loo.

Clutching a roll of paper, I gingerly negotiated the slippery slope leading up to the little shed. Balancing uncomfortably and supporting myself on my thighs, which had already begun to quiver with exertion, I held my breath and prayed for swift deliverance. My prayers were answered, but as I shifted my weight minutely to reach for the loo paper, the whole platform collapsed. Sheer panic saved me from an unspeakably disgusting fate. As I was falling, I grabbed one of the overhead beams and hung there, my feet inches from the bottom of the pit, yelling for help. Deo, who by now was well used to the sound of my voice, came rushing to the rescue and, managing to keep a suitably solemn expression on his face, extracted his boss from a hideous predicament. Muttering my thanks, I clambered down awkwardly and was horrified to hear a burst of suppressed giggles: the accident had been witnessed, in all its glorious detail, by two young girls who lived next door. I thanked Manu's nephew and apologised for wrecking his loo, and hurried down to the jetty where the others were waiting.

The boats were loaded and it was time to leave. Waving goodbye to a few bored Asmatters, who stopped picking their noses for a moment to wave back, we fell into the mud one last time and boarded the canoes. Turning right, we left Agats in a swirl of muddy spray and headed up-river into the unknown.

I gazed at the broad reaches ahead, swept with a feeling of intense euphoria and relief, similar to the high a convict must feel on his release as the prison doors swing closed behind him. The wind and spray caressed us, carrying the intoxicating smell of the jungle. Fane and I behaved like Japanese tourists, the motor-drives of our cameras clicking and chattering as we took endless dull shots of each other and of distant rain-swept river banks, while Don, the old professional, smiled indulgently at the juvenile antics of his travelling companions and saved his precious film.

We soon turned into a narrower river where the noise of the engine echoed eerily off the banks, causing clouds of fruit-bats to erupt, shrieking, from the trees. The supply boat was some way behind. We decided to stop at a small village called Warse. Clambering ashore, we were quickly surrounded by a crowd of T-shirted individuals loudly crying out for tobacco. Piet distributed a few sticks and Fane and I wandered around the village, but found it dull. Don, however, became hyperactive, organising with Piet's help groups of emaciated old women to pose in the doorways of their ramshackle huts, cackling hysterically each time the shutter fell.

Fane and I were enticed by the sound of woodcutting to follow a muddy path through a green tunnel of palm trees. We emerged into a small clearing to find an aged man, squatting amid a pile of wood-shavings, working on the prow of a canoe. A few deft, sure movements and the intricate image of a cockatoo began to appear. On our way back we were accosted by a man who wanted us to buy his pet pig; he became very angry when we declined. I spotted a young man afflicted with a severe squint. He was flattered when I asked if I might take his picture. Shortly afterwards a small boy, clutching an equally small bow and arrow, tapped my hand and explained that he was a great hunter; for a few rupiah he would be pleased to shoot a bird for me. I accepted his challenge and, with astonishing skill, he startled a pigeon that was perched in a tree a few feet above us. I paid him all the same. Suddenly, from the river, we heard the supply boat chugging past. Ignoring the cries of 'rokok lagi' (more tobacco), we set off in pursuit.

The afternoon brought violent changes of weather. One moment we would be roasting in the blazing sun, the next desperately seeking our waterproofs as chilling downpours drenched us. As yet, we were still landlubbers. Our awkward movements would cause the canoe to lurch dangerously and wake Joseph, forcing him into frantic action at the controls as he attempted to avoid capsizing. We would have to learn to predict the rapid changes in weather. Fortunately, Don was quite a reliable yardstick: the moment he thought the sun might shine, the air would be filled with the smell of Ambre Solaire.

The Jet tributary met the narrow, winding Powet River,

which forced its way between vegetation so dense that it seemed almost to struggle for its own survival. Progress was slow, impeded by the giant yellow stems of bamboo clumps which stuck out into the water. We were dazzled by the multi-coloured orchids that clung to the trunks of immensely tall trees. There was a sudden abundance of bird life: startled egrets flapped clumsily away, herons gazed idly at us from the safety of the river bank, while cockatoos screeched from the tree-tops.

The colour of the water had changed too. It was much darker, and occasionally a strange yet familiar smell hung in the air. Noticing our curiosity, Piet told us it was oil; in places you could see it bubbling blackly to the surface. I wondered how long this paradise might be allowed to exist before the developers moved in. Farther on, Fane noticed several round objects floating in the water. He asked Piet what they were and then, turning to me, told me they were some kind of jungle fruit, similar to an orange. Why didn't I try one? Without hesitating, I scooped one out of the water and took a large bite. Peals of sadistic mirth met my reaction, as I spat out the disgusting pulp; they were not oranges at all, but some foul (probably highly poisonous) seeds that had fallen from the overhanging trees.

The intimacy of the lush Powet was soon left behind. We were now heading upstream along the vast Sirets River, which in places was almost half a mile wide. This should lead us into the area known as the Upper Sirets, where we hoped to make contact with the orang hutan.

Due to the dangers of driftwood and submerged logs, the crew refused to travel at night, and so before dark we stopped at the village of Jaosokor. For a small contribution, apparently to the school community, we commandeered the school teacher's house for our first night on the river. Inside, it was pitch dark, and our able crew could not get the pressure lamp to work. With considerable difficulty we erected our mosquito nets; Don and I thought it wise to allow Fane to construct the Great Bed of Ware first, to avoid certain injury from the ropes which were soon to criss-cross the small room. We were further inhibited by the presence of the entire village, who had crowded in to watch us open-mouthed. Their curiosity reached fever-pitch when Fane, clad in an elegantly tied sarong, started to inflate his bright red Lilo with the aid of a small foot pump. As the Lilo billowed into shape, the villagers began to shout at the top of their voices and stamp their feet so forcefully that Deo quickly ushered them out, though one or two villagers resisted, peering back to catch a last glimpse of the miracle.

Deo came back, shaking his head and muttering, 'Bloody jungle johnnies! Stupid, not like Batak tribe.'

The episode was exhausting after a long first day on the river, and we were starving. Soon the boys had a fire blazing outside, and a great pot of rice was on the boil. One of the villagers had offered us a couple of evil-smelling catfish and a stringy old chicken, but his price was too high. However, Deo soon had Fane and me tucking into great platefuls of rice topped with fried eggs. I didn't bother to ask from where he had procured them. Don's meal took rather longer to prepare to his satisfaction. One of the mysterious silver packages had been produced from the depths of his rucksack (I believe it was turkey flavour that night) and Deo was issued with strict cooking instructions. His first two attempts were sent back to the kitchen, but after persevering he was finally complimented. We were all relieved to see Don happy with his food.

Hot tea, sweetened with Fane's bountiful supply of Hermesetas – probably the most useful item we had brought – induced total exhaustion and we gratefully crawled under our nets. Unhappily, sleep did not descend immediately due to the infernal noise next door. Pak Polici had taken a great liking to my wireless and had borrowed it for the evening. It seemed that our crew were holding some kind of Indonesian jamboree. Don padded next door and roared at the party to keep quiet. There was deadly silence.

We awoke hours later to the deafening roar of torrential rain. I had never before experienced such a downpour. The noise as it crashed down forced us to shout at one another over our breakfast. The river was scarcely visible. Peering out of the hut, I just managed to make out the blurred figures of Joseph and Alphonse trying to bail out the canoes. I could foresee an extremely wet journey up-river to Senggo, where we had arranged to collect extra fuel.

Cocooned in the strange plastic world of my poncho, I sat staring at my feet and became alarmed to notice how quickly they were being covered by the filthy water that sloshed around in the bottom of the canoe. As if the rain wasn't enough, we had sprung a leak and water was now bursting through the mud-filled seams. I silently cursed Joseph as the jolly awning sprang to mind, and turned round to see how the others were faring. Piet seemed oblivious to the rain. He sat perched in his normal position on one of the large fuel drums, rivulets of water streaming down his impassive face, only occasionally shaking himself briskly, like a dog, whipping a fine arc of spray around him. Fane was asleep, a shapeless blob under his waterproof, while Don resembled Chay Blythe rounding the Horn, resplendent in his bright blue heavy-weather sailing anorak, and repeatedly checking the sky for improvement. The only sign of wildlife was a rather large lizard lying on the bank which, on closer inspection turned out to be our first crocodile. It looked as miserable and unimpressed as we were.

Joseph reduced speed. Turning round, I could just distinguish the outline of a small village on the distant bank. Piet's suggestion that we should stop to take shelter seemed like a good idea. As we approached, the village longhouse began to take shape through the curtain of rain, a building about fifty yards long, rising on sturdy posts ten feet off the ground. Alerted by the sound of our engines, a few dark figures emerged from inside and stood silently staring as we clawed our way up the muddy bank. In order to gain access to the hut we had to climb an almost vertical pole which was as slippery as an eel and, apart from the odd notch cut out of its length, lacked proper footholds. The ascent was frustrating and painful, but at least provided entertainment for the villagers and created a friendly atmosphere, for our clumsy efforts were met with appreciative laughter.

We tumbled into a dark interior, so smoky that immediately our eyes began to smart. With tears running down my face, I squinted into the gloom and gradually blurred shapes began to materialise around me, drifting in and out of focus like spirits. We were surprised to find ourselves in the midst of a great number of people, most of whom were half-naked and squatting around small open fires. As we stared, one group moved away from their fire in silent invitation; soon we were warm and enveloped in clouds of steam as our soaking clothes began to dry.

These friendly people gave us the freedom of their dwelling, and we wandered around cautiously stepping on the strips of bark covering the bamboo floor which bounced alarmingly underfoot. Several large war-shields emblazoned with bold geometric designs were piled on the floor; I was relieved to find them cocooned in a mesh of cobwebs, suggesting that the village had been at peace for some time. I spotted two yellowing human thigh bones, stuck haphazardly into the wall – perhaps the coveted relics of a great chief, or the leftovers of a feast. Surrounding each fireplace was a solid wooden frame that appeared to be the main support for the roof, and jutting out of each were intricately carved wooden effigies, rather like totem poles, depicting figures contorted into what I thought were highly erotic postures. Piet explained that they were in fact headhunting symbols. He told me that these were ancestor poles, dedicated to the souls of the decapitated warriors who were captured in inter-tribal headhunting raids. These poles, carved from the roots of mangrove trees, were only made when the *Kepala Perang* (War Chief) decided that it was time to rally his people and seek revenge.

Yellow slabs of sunlight were cutting into the gloom through the entrances: the rain had stopped. Back in the canoe Fane and I decided to celebrate the change in the weather by raiding the biscuit tin, but our clumsy rustlings alerted Don.

'Get out of there,' he growled, slamming the lid back on. 'These are emergency rations – and I don't see any emergency as yet.'

We had come to realise that Don had a secret dread of running out of food, and it was becoming increasingly difficult to whip anything from under his beady eye.

Several hours later we stopped at Waganu, a crocodile-hunting village, partly to trade for skins but more urgently to relieve ourselves. Under the hot and fascinated stare of a man with a human knuckle-bone stuck through his nose, it proved rather difficult to perform, but finally, with great aplomb, and synchronisation, we delighted him with three strong, bright yellow jets – exaggerated in colour due to the vitamin pills we were taking.

No crocodile skins were to be seen, so we pushed on to Senggo, a large village situated off the Sirets on a tributary of the Wildeman River. It spread over a considerable area which had been hacked out of the jungle, and boasted a church, a mission, a few stores and an airstrip, whose windsock we could see hanging impotently from a pole. The village itself had the atmosphere of a frontier town, a place beyond which lay the unknown.

We were to spend the night in one of the village stores. Built over a side-water, its wooden exterior bleached almost white, it was a place of some charm, and afforded us fine views of the smooth brown river sweeping past just outside. The owner was asking an exorbitant amount in return for the use of a couple of his storerooms, but soon relented after Deo had applied some effective bullying. The rooms were filled with sacks of rice and cartons of washing powder, but one contained the unexpected luxury of an old lumpy bed. I won the toss. Water was lapping against the posts beneath us, and already a steady stream of mosquitoes eager for fresh blood was erupting from the cracks in the floorboards. Grabbing towels and soap, we hurried to the river.

The water was cool and refreshing, quickly dissolving the

weariness and filth of the previous two days. It was a relief to exercise our cramped limbs as we battled against the powerful current. Later, we sat drying off on a half-submerged log, watching the suffused light of the dying sun turn everything to gold around us.

Feeling clean and respectable we set off through the village to visit the mission. Our efforts at the river were wasted: the mud-packed path under our bare feet was like an ice-rink, and standing upright was practically impossible for more than a few steps. A small stream flowed on each side of the path, and old women, poling slender canoes, cackled at our predicament as they slid past in the gloom. We stopped to rest at a small store. The owner was chatting to a young woman whose hour-glass figure was squeezed into an old cocktail dress. As she leant over the counter, we were provided with an excellent view of a pair of smooth brown thighs. Flashing us a salacious smile, she tried in broken English to interest us in some eggs. As Fane politely declined, her provocative glance lingered longer than necessary over his tall figure.

Slipping and sliding, we struggled on, eventually arriving at the mission looking dishevelled, and dreading the polished atmosphere we had found in Agats. We were pleasantly surprised.

A great roar of 'enter' followed our polite knock at the door. The first thing I noticed was a large table littered with empty Johnnie Walker whisky bottles and blackened with cigarette burns.

Propped up on this table were four bare feet belonging to two gentlemen in their mid-fifties, sprawled in battered chairs. Strong horny hands pumped ours, and cats were hastily kicked off to accommodate us, while ice-cold cans of foaming lager and fat Indonesian cigars were thrust into our hands. These engaging missionaries were clad in baggy shorts and T-shirts, one of them bearing the slogan *'God is good, but Fosters is better'*. One was Austrian, the other Dutch, but both had been ordained in 1951 at Mill Hill in London and had spent most of

10 First encounter with primitive people

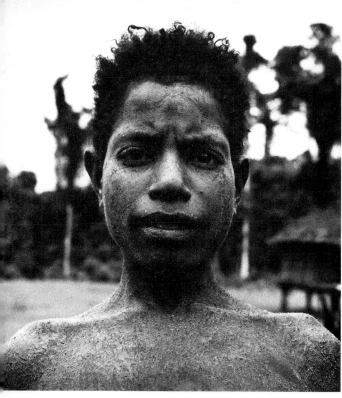

11 *Left*, a young girl
afflicted with
Frambrosia

13 & 14 *Opposite*,
riverside trading:
Piet (*below*)
was far more
expert than the
amateurs Shand
and Fane (*above*)

12 *Below*, mother and
daughter, early
morning by the Brassa
River

15 Calling to the orang hutan

16 A startled response from inside the hut

their lives in Indonesia. They were in Borneo during the Emergency, were thrown in jail a few times, and had spent the last fifteen years here in Senggo. Listening to them speak it was clear that they felt a genuine love for the country, while regarding life with a certain amount of cynicism. They restored my waning faith in missionaries.

They were enthusiastic to hear about our expedition, reckoning we had a fifty-fifty chance of encountering the orang hutan and similar odds of getting into trouble. We pored over beautiful hand-drawn maps of the area, made by their predecessors, from which we gained a much clearer impression of the river system. They pointed out likely places to find the orang hutan, and showed us the location of the most recent sighting. We were surprised to see how close to the Brassa River we were already.

'No problem,' they said. 'You kick the backside of the crew and they get you there by tomorrow evening.'

Clearly, Manu Lamera had slightly exaggerated the distances back in Merauke; any reluctance by our crew to push on would mean extra days and therefore extra money for him . . . Our fuel had been organised and would be delivered in Woowi, a village on the Sirets, saving us the diversion to Senggo on our return.

I couldn't keep my eyes off the empty whisky bottles. Apart from the rows standing on the table, there were scores more strewn liberally around the room.

Reading my thoughts, the Austrian said, 'Sorry, friend. We're fresh out of the hard stuff. That bastard policeman has impounded our latest delivery, and we refuse to pay the duty he has slapped on it. After all,' he laughed, 'we're living in a dry area!'

His colleague warned us that the policeman would probably try to confiscate our passports before we left, forcing us to return to Senggo to collect them, and expecting a little 'oleh-oleh' (present) for their safe-keeping.

'The key to this bugger,' he continued, 'is his wife. Get around her and he'll be putty in your hands.'

We interrupted to tell him about the interesting young lady we had met in the store. The missionary laughed and confirmed her identity.

'She's a hot little number,' he said, 'known locally as Evil Augustine!'

The flood of Fosters had dried up and, not wishing to impose further on their generous hospitality, we left. The black night and beer on an empty stomach made the return journey no easier; all three of us managed to crash into one of the streams. Deo had cooked up a storm – Fane and I indulged in a treat tonight: onions and sardines, while Don tucked into yet another silver package. We decided to send the Batak to deal with the policeman tomorrow, and Fane volunteered to exert his charm on Evil Augustine, if it was really necessary.

CHAPTER SEVEN

Edge of Nowhere

The mosquitoes found a chink in Don's net that night. The following morning his body was a mass of red lumps and one swollen eyelid was half-closed. I was not in great shape either, being afflicted with a severe bout of constipation. The sun rose to find me wobbling precariously at the top of a ladder which was propped against the back of the hut, but my condition was not easily rectified as I was obliged to retreat inside every time a canoe passed, in order not to offend the occupants with the sight of a large white backside. Our well-stocked medical kit could offer remedies for every ailment apart from my own, so I penned an SOS to our friends at the mission.

Deo had visited the policeman, who was magnanimously allowing us to keep our passports while insisting we leave behind our *Surat Jalan*. As a high rate of literacy seems unlikely among the jungle people, we agreed to this, especially as we could avoid paying *oleh-oleh* by sending Deo to collect the document on our return. He was dispatched to deliver the *Surat Jalan* and also my note to the missionaries; he would follow later in the supply canoe.

Progress was painfully slow: the engine was suffering from an ailment similar to my own. By mid-afternoon we had hiccoughed into a dull little village whose sole item of interest was a baby cassowary that skittered after us like a tame puppy. I persuaded Don to hold the bird while I took a photograph: it promptly shat all over him.

It was only two-thirty, but our decision to press on was met with howls of protest from Joseph and Piet, who insisted that we could not reach the next village before nightfall. Ignoring these Fabian tactics, we ordered immediate embarkation.

At that moment the supply canoe came whipping round the bend in a sheet of spray. Balanced like a figurehead in the prow was Deo, proudly holding aloft two catfish that glistened in the sunlight. They had stopped a passing canoe and he had traded the fish for one of his bright yellow pencils. I asked whether the missionaries had given him anything for me. He mumbled that they were not there so he had given the note to a boy to deliver. I suspected he was deterred by the long slippery path. Apart from the catfish, a fully grown cassowary lay trussed like a turkey in the bottom of the canoe, a gift to this village from someone in Senggo. Realising it was destined for the pot, the bird suddenly made a last desperate bid for freedom, scattering Alphonse and Pak Polici with fierce slashings of its long horny legs. After some difficulty it was retrussed, restoring casserole of cassowary to that night's menu.

By the time we finally set off we were highly irritable; imagine our surprise when, barely two hours later, another village appeared. Piet at least had the decency to mumble an apology, while Joseph merely scowled, refusing to meet with our withering glares. The mutual trust we had built up had almost disintegrated. Fane coldly requested a few words with Piet later on.

It was a pity that bad feelings marred our arrival at Bourbis, as it was the most charming village. We set up camp in the schoolhouse, where Fane and I took advantage of the wide verandah to test our hammocks for the first time. After a couple of abortive attempts, we were swaying contentedly, regally ordering Deo to bring cups of tea while we surveyed the sweeping panorama. Don eyed us enviously from his position on the hard floorboards. Some time later, Deo produced a slimy and tasteless mess of catfish, which we forced down, spitting out hundreds of razor-sharp bones. We needed all the protein we could get.

A gigantic full moon loomed over the river, and the silence was complete save for the continuous croaking of the bullfrogs. We summoned our crew. In order to instil the required element of fear, Fane, Don and I argued heatedly among ourselves for several minutes. Don reinforced each statement by crashing his fist down on to one of the tin boxes, causing the boys to jump in alarm. Deo translated word for word with the force and panache of a born actor.

From now on, we informed the crew, we wanted to know every detail of the route, how long each part of the journey would take and where we were going to stop. It was essential that we should push on as hard as possible to maximise our chances of meeting the orang hutan. We had not come all this way to be exploited by idiots. If we found any cause for complaint the mission would be informed on our return and Manu Lamera would not be paid. From their expressions it was clear that even they could comprehend that an unpaid boss meant unpaid crew. Money was obviously the key. Piet, their spokesman, solemnly assured us that everything would now be 'bagus sekali' (very good). Joseph went so far as to unbend his scowling features into a flashy brick-toothed grin and to pledge his willingness to go alone into the jungle and personally drag out the orang hutan. He arranged the map between us on the floor and we peered at his finger as it crept up the sheet. First, he suggested, we should proceed as far as we could up the Brassa River. Failing that, we would try the Kolff and then, if time allowed, we would head south-east to negotiate the Becking River. To show our approval of his plan we distributed cigarettes, and secretly wondered how long these good intentions would last.

Much later, under the canopy of my net, I switched on my torch and reached for a cigarette. I was surprised to find, wedged between the tinfoil and the edge of the packet, several local roll-ups. Perhaps this was a peace offering.

The atmosphere next morning was charged with anticipation and excitement. Even the crew seemed affected: for once they were efficient and eager to set off. As we hurried down to the canoes the first sharp rays of sunlight cut through the clouds, hitting the dew-drenched jungle; it was as if a giant jewel-case had been suddenly opened. A strong sweet smell hung in the air, so pungent it took my breath away.

The supply canoe carried an extra passenger, a boy named Zacchius. He attended the school in Bourbis and was to ride with us as far as a village on the Kolff River to visit his sick mother. Piet was keen to take him, as the boy would be able to translate local dialects, but I disliked him on sight. He was insolent and had an overdeveloped lower lip that quivered pinkly and pet-ulantly when he spoke. I was determined not to let his arrival ruin what promised to be a splendid day, and I soon forgot about him when the river began to unfold ahead of us.

As the supply canoe drew alongside, I yelled to Deo through the hiss of spray that if he kept the rain gods at bay I would buy him a whore in Jakarta.

'No problem, *Harimau!*' he shouted back.

Arms stretching towards the sky and fists clenched, he closed his eyes, threw back his head and broke loudly into Batak song, startling a pair of white cockatoos which swooped away, screeching loudly in outrage.

We arrived at a confluence of rivers. With a dramatic gesture, Joseph turned the canoe and announced, 'Brassa'.

I sensed immediately that the Brassa was a friendly river; it seemed almost protective towards us. I felt we were being drawn by some strong force into its luxuriant domain, like a broody hen tucking her young under a wing. It was oddly reassuring and the roar of the engines became almost an embarrassment as they violated the serenity. After a while the river widened and on the distant right-hand bank we saw the long shapes of canoes resting in the shallows. As we approached, a few dark figures emerged from the ramshackle huts. We had arrived at Piramanak.

A crowd gathered to watch. Eager to record our first encounter with primitive people, we scrambled ashore, brandishing cameras. The women took exception to our clumsy behaviour, hurrying back to their dwellings, breasts flying in all directions.

Piet warned us to move slowly. He swiftly took control by distributing sticks of tobacco among the men. A few minutes later the women sidled back. What a weird group they were. The men were completely naked while the women modestly wore minute G-strings woven from coarse brown grass and attached to rattan waistbands. These might have looked wonderfully sensual on Copacabana Beach, but on these women they caused no sudden stirring of the loins. Their stomachs were extremely distended and their bodies disfigured by patches of scaly flaking skin. The men were no better looking, though any porn king would have been delighted to employ them. Some had pushed the shafts of their penises up into their scrotums and tied the ends of the foreskins with palm fronds. Elephantiasis had swollen their testicles to enormous proportions, the glands standing out like bunches of grapes. One unfortunate man could hardly move, so enlarged were his limbs by an advanced state of this appalling disease.

Using Zacchius as interpreter, we inquired whether they possessed any stone axes, but all they could show us were a few broken bows and arrows. Don produced his enormous camera and was soon busy taking portraits. Tempers flared when he yelled at Fane and me to keep out of the way: apparently our filthy T-shirts kept edging into his viewfinder. Since he was hogging all the best material we thought this most unfair, but I consoled myself by fitting on my long lens and zooming on less artistic subjects. I could already visualise the sensation my exhibition would cause back in London; it would be entitled 'Studies of the Private Parts of the Primitive People' . . . It was only after I had finished three rolls of film that I noticed the camera was switched off. Finally, the maestro announced the end of the session with his models and, as trading was quiet, we returned to the canoes.

The heat was by now unbearable and the scorching wind flayed our faces like a razor. Lunch was a rare treat. With impressive foresight we had bought in London a quantity of powdered soup, ranging from plain chicken to more exotic mulligatawny. That morning we had filled a thermos with hot water, and now sat sipping boiling hot soup under a boiling hot sun. Though incongruous, it was surprisingly good and would, no doubt, become a daily ritual.

★

The farther up-river we went, the more black, naked and primitive the people became. From a distance we could see a tiny figure standing on a steep bank, dwarfed by the height of his rickety old hut which stood behind him on ridiculously slender posts. He was gesticulating madly, indicating something that gleamed red in the sun. Drawing closer it turned out to be a magnificent shield, similar to those we had seen in the longhouse a few days earlier, but infinitely more impressive. Its surface was carved with wild looping patterns, and had been stained red and white, probably by the juice of some root. Clearly the man was anxious to trade. Four naked women had by now tumbled like lazy sloths from their dwelling, and stood in a group behind him on the bank. He was a most ingenuous character, tiny in stature apart from one part of his anatomy, which would come in useful considering the size of his harem. He wore a necklace of yellowing tusks and brightly coloured seeds, while across his thighs ran deep puckered scars – perhaps the result of a gory tussle with a giant pig.

His eyes lit up at the sight of our gleaming parangs. I would have been happy to exchange one for his shield but Piet insisted that a few coils of fishing line and some hooks would be enough. The man resolutely shook his head. Deo was equally determined to have the shield and entered into fierce negotiation, using Zacchius as interpreter. Yet another coil of fishing line was added to our side of the deal, but the tough little trader remained defiant. With a flash of inspiration, Deo tore off his T-shirt and waved it in front of him. A smile spread across the man's face and he thrust the shield into Deo's hands. We still had a lot to learn about trading.

One of the women was suffering from a hideous burn that

stretched from elbow to wrist. Her arm was already as dark and swollen as a ripe plum and oozing pus; the thick, sweet smell of infection was nauseating – gangrene had set in. Don dressed the wound and gently bandaged her arm. She mewed pathetically with pain, and I now fully comprehended the fragility of life in these remote areas.

We were all dog-tired by late afternoon when we pulled into the village of Pattitipi. This was the most remote settled encampment known to exist on the Brassa; from here on we could expect everything or nothing. Fane remarked that the people we had encountered that day were far more primitive than we had foreseen, and he could scarcely imagine what to expect from the orang hutan – if we ever managed to find them. Before we left the canoes, Piet warned us to go carefully in this village. Only two years ago the first attempt at contact was made by the outside world, but the people ran away in fright. A second attempt six months later was equally unsuccessful. Warfare was still part of everyday life: they would fight over anything from a woman to a sago tree. Piet was told in Senggo that there had been a killing here just a few weeks ago. He pointedly ignored my inane comment that there could be a skull knocking around, and advised us to sleep lightly that night – though, as an added precaution, one of the crew would stay awake.

As I knew from past experience that Indonesians are physically incapable of insomnia, I resolved not to hit the pill bottle that night. A few naked emaciated villagers watched as we crawled up the bank, eyeing us in disconcerting silence. We assured each other that they seemed friendly enough. One had paralysed legs, and propelled himself along with amazing agility, using odd jerking movements of his arms.

Though spartan, our accommodation was delightfully picturesque: a tiny deserted shack, situated on the river bank, reassuringly near the canoes in case it became necessary to beat a hasty retreat. Access was provided by a crudely made ladder, its struts bound together with strips of bark. Being cautious, we invited the boys to go first – after all, they were lighter than us. They quickly clambered up, closely followed by the rotund Batak. He had almost reached the top when a strut snapped with a great crack, sending him hurtling to the ground. Blood spurted from a deep gash on the back of his thigh. Trying not to laugh, we managed to heave him up between us. We conquered the ladder without further injury and I turned my expert attention to Deo's wound.

Secretly I was pleased to have the opportunity to put into practice the knowledge I had acquired in London. Ordering my patient to lie on his front, I laid out my medical kit. I cleaned the gash and sprinkled it with antibiotic powder, but was disappointed to see it did not require stitching. However, I noticed an excess of loose skin hanging around the wound. It was time for the scalpel. Don had been watching my efforts rather doubtfully, and now caught sight of the mad gleam in my eye. Hastily grabbing the scalpel, he insisted this was not really necessary. With a dexterity any GP would have envied, I slapped on a dressing and stood back to admire my handiwork. The patient was warned to keep his leg dry for a few days. If infection set in I would be forced to use 'Rambo'. He thanked me politely but gave me a wide berth for some time.

After the operation we prepared our sleeping quarters. We propped an old bamboo door against the entrance for extra security. It wasn't much, but it would creak if an intruder attempted to creep in during the night. Fane and I chose to remain dirty rather than brave the ladder again, but Don disappeared down to the river to wash, only to reappear shortly, having been attacked by some vicious underwater creature that had stung his arm and stained the skin a curious yellow. I was happy to offer my services, but he firmly declined.

Meanwhile, the dreadful Zacchius was finally being made to pay his way, pendulous lip trembling with exertion as he used the foot pump to inflate the Lilos. My loathing increasing by the second, I suggested that in future they hide it and let him blow them up.

Peering down, I noticed what looked like a fully armed war party assembling around the base of the shack. Convinced an attack was imminent, I yelled an order to 'repel boarders!' It was embarrassing to discover the group had merely come to trade. In no time they had shinned up the ladder and were arranging their wares on the bamboo floor, which was sagging alarmingly beneath our combined weight. Fane immediately spotted a fine stone axe-head and, before I could intervene, had secured it in exchange for a parang. I was furious, obliged to settle for a pair of rather inferior spears tipped with sharpened cassowary bone. Don left us to it, preferring to wait until we visited the Asmat tribes in the coastal areas to pick up a sculpture. Trading completed, and fearing the floor was about to collapse, we summoned Piet, who tactfully dismissed our visitors with promises of more trade the next day. They slipped away like black shadows, leaving a peculiarly unpleasant and rank odour in their wake.

Don, who had been checking through our inventory, suddenly announced that he thought we had 'lost' a few items. After a thorough search, we found that not only an axe-head and two T-shirts, but an entire box of tobacco had gone astray. We yelled for the boys. A second careful search took place, but to no avail. Some thieving bastard was enjoying the benefits of a very lucrative cache. We agreed the goods had probably been lifted in Jaosokor, the place where we had spent the first night. I remembered it well: the mass of villagers crowding into that dark hut – it would have been so easy. Nobody was specifically to blame, but we made it clear that in future the crew must be more vigilant. Tobacco was absolutely vital to the success of our expedition; without it, life could become dangerous.

Deo managed to produce a reasonable dinner, though Fane and I were beginning to tire of sardines and rice. We ignored Don, who was drooling over another of his silver packages. The meal was accompanied by the BBC World Service. Reception on my wireless was good for once and the tinny chimes of Big Ben rolled out over the jungle, to be followed by the perfectly modulated voice of the newscaster announcing that England had beaten Australia in the third Test.

A scrabbling outside announced the arrival of a visitor. Peering into the darkness, we made out the twisted features of the cripple we had seen earlier. He was hauling himself up the ladder with the dexterity of a monkey. Once inside, he sat quietly in a corner and we forgot about him until an odd slapping sound attracted our attention.

Turning round to investigate, Don exclaimed, 'Take a butcher's at this – you won't believe it!'

The little figure was hunched over, gazing open-mouthed at us, his hands a blur of activity in his lap . . . It was rather embarrassing and we were unsure whether to feel revolted or flattered. We stopped staring to enable him to finish. After a few seconds we heard a stifled grunt and he swung away down the ladder to disappear into the night.

Piet had been conspicuously absent during the latter half of the evening, and arrived back with good news. In the village he had found out that the orang hutan had been sighted about two hours up-river. They had constructed a makeshift hut on a high bank, and there were signs that they were still there. Piet negotiated the services of the man who had sighted them: in exchange for some tobacco he would be willing to act as a guide.

A violent rainstorm during the night punched a great hole in the roof, soaking us to the skin. Fane bore the brunt of this downpour as his net was positioned directly under the yawning gap.

A light rain was still falling in the morning and the river was almost completely shrouded in a veil of wispy vapour. The stillness of dawn was disturbed only by our snoring crew – exhausted, no doubt, by their night-long vigil! The Batak, however, was up early. I was surprised to find him crouching by the makings of a fire, gently coaxing the damp wood to burn. His face was unusually pallid; he mournfully explained that he was 'sakit sekali' (very sick) and had not slept. I examined his leg, causing him considerable discomfort by slowly peeling off the plaster. The wound was hot and puffy, but not infected, so I changed the dressing and assured him he would live.

We kicked and chivvied the boys out of their somnolent mood. We were eager to get going. A few villagers had already gathered outside, clutching an assortment of wares in the hope of further trading, but they were going to be out of luck. In the pale watery light they looked hardly human, and one of them was making short work of a long piece of sugar cane. Biting into one end, he ripped off the green bark with vicious twists of his head and then shredded the sticky stalk with a powerful sawing of his teeth. It was like watching a carrot being pushed into a blender. All the while, one eye was cocked as a warning to us to keep our distance, like a dog with a bone. It was an act of such animal savagery that it caused me to shiver involuntarily and I became instantly aware that we were through the veneer of civilisation and firmly in touch with barbarism.

As we climbed down the ladder to make our way to the river, we glimpsed two or three figures under the hut sifting through our refuse, like hens on a garbage dump. We realised we should have burnt our rubbish as we watched them pick up the discarded film packets, smell them, then pop them into their mouths and chew contentedly. Even worse – and I didn't stop to see the outcome – one of them had salvaged the bloody dressing from Deo's leg . . .

CHAPTER EIGHT

Orang Hutan

As we set off up-river the first rays of sunlight were beginning to dispel the vapour that enveloped us in a swirling grey cloak. Motionless in the prow of the canoe sat our guide from Pattitipi, his eyes glued to the green wall of forest that slid silently past. Tiny drops of moisture beaded the rattan hoops hanging from his earlobes; they sparkled brilliantly where the sun touched them, like diamond-encrusted ear-rings. Flocks of green and yellow parakeets swooped low over the river, while high overhead flew hornbills, unhurrying as driven pheasants.

The temperature soared well into the hundreds. To keep ourselves occupied as we sweltered on our tin boxes we checked and rechecked the camera equipment. I made sure that mine was turned on today. Time dragged intolerably, but, after two hours, we swept round a long bend in the river and our guide came to life, motioning to Joseph to cut the engines. The canoe coasted forward in silence. On the left-hand side of the river rose a steep muddy bank at least twenty feet high, and balanced at the top was a large raised tumbledown dwelling. It appeared to be totally deserted until we noticed the thin curl of blue smoke drifting from the roof and a few crudely carved canoes in the shallows. Our guide was now standing on the prow and producing an odd hooting sound from between his cupped hands. At first nothing happened. He called again; a dog started barking. We were now extremely close, almost beneath the lip of the bank, and the blinding sun was directly in our eyes. The guide called again and quite suddenly a figure appeared, then another. Had it not been for the slight blur of movement, I would not have noticed them. They blended perfectly into the background and remained motionless. The guide shouted a few words to them. One replied; a tentative conversation began. In the canoe, we could scarcely contain our impatience as the sun grew hotter and the flies descended on us. At last, a satisfied grunt concluded the conversation; we were welcome.

Don, Fane and I launched ourselves simultaneously from the canoe and stumbled up the slope, cursing our clumsiness as we slipped repeatedly. Don, showing the agility of experience, was up the long notched pole of the hut like shit off a shovel. He ducked inside and instantly reappeared with a yell.

'You won't believe this!'

My heart started hammering: I was close behind, and peered into the darkness. A few maddening seconds passed while my eyes adjusted to the gloom. Then a sort of Brueghel tableau unfurled before me. The interior was densely criss-crossed with fine lances of sunlight which filtered through every chink in the framework and, like spotlights, pinpointed the frozen positions of the startled inhabitants. There was total silence; a hundred pairs of eyes gleamed. I caught Fane's sharp intake of breath as he joined us. We were transported thousands of years back in time, into another world. Then the thin wail of a child broke the tension. Gingerly we edged farther inside, bending double to avoid the low bamboo rafters that were draped with fishing nets. Slender longbows were propped against the walls; a yellowing bone gleamed dully on the floor. Perhaps we had moved too soon. Some of the males and younger children were already beginning to slip out of the exit at the other end, while the women turned away, covering themselves and the babies at their breasts with blankets of woodbark. Only a few men, their bodies daubed grey with the ash that had drifted across the entire floor, approached us cautiously. One of them gently squeezed my arm.

Piet and the boys had brought with them a box of tobacco and several bags of salt, which we distributed among the people. Gradually their confidence grew. Even the women became bolder. They shed their bark blankets and suckled their babies. Thin mangy dogs emerged from the shadows and nosed through the rubbish, trying to avoid the thumps which would send them yelping back into the corners. The people seemed to split naturally into family units, each of which had an allotted space around a small fireplace. The children wailed constantly. I saw three babies fighting over one nipple, while a small puppy hung happily on the other. Many of the women were missing their little fingers: apparently they hacked them off if they lost a child at birth. Both sexes wore nose and ear ornaments. The women looked particularly strange, almost feral, with the long waving whiskers of bone that protruded horizontally from their nostrils. The children wore necklaces of pigs' teeth and shells, while the men's biceps were tightly circled with rattan armbands. These, I discovered, were somehow used in lighting fires. Some of the men and older boys had tied their foreskins with strips of palm fibre, in the same way as the villagers at Piramanak, while on others the penis hung naturally. I wondered if they tied them like this to prevent insects crawling inside.

Apart from an unpleasant skin disease which covers most of the body in flaking dry skin, and the odd case of latent elephantiasis, they looked remarkably fit, more robust than the village people we had met so far. Perhaps a nomadic way of life is more desirable than a settled one; I suspect that all the people in this area were once as healthy as these, deteriorating only as outside contact increased. I wondered how long the orang hutan would survive. Certainly we were not helping to stem the tide. We had already dished out a few T-shirts, and the chief was now the proud owner of a pair of shiny satin shorts. Using our guide as interpreter, we asked for stone axes and were shown two. One was beautiful, its stone blade smooth and unblemished and its handle intricately carved. The owner wasn't interested in parting with it, even in exchange for two steel axes, which seemed odd. I managed to procure the other stone axe, though it was smaller and its blade was pitted and chipped.

17 The orang hutan – dignity and simplicity

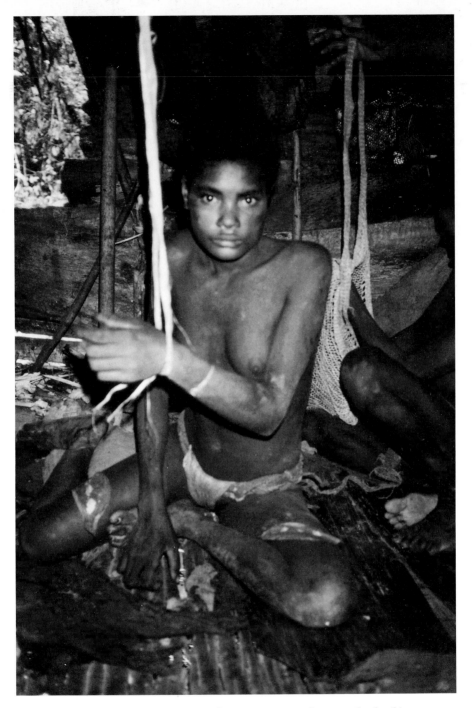

19 *Above*, such helpless beauty – the young orang hutan who had been bitten by a snake

18 *Left*, inside the orang hutan bivouac they stared at us in astonishment

20 The orang hutan guide

21 Distributing the visitors' gifts

Explaining that we wanted to take photographs was an extremely difficult task, even for our guide. As we extracted the cameras the people crowded round, making clucking noises with their tongues, completely mystified. The hut was so gloomy that a flash was necessary. Don could get no reading at all on his light meter, and my camera was the only one with a flash attachment. The first blinding sheet of light caused mixed reactions. The older children immediately made for the exit, the women once again disappeared beneath their bark blankets, but the men howled with delight. The whirring noise of the flash recharging and the little red light winking on and off were equally popular. We cursed ourselves for neglecting to bring a Polaroid camera. Meanwhile, Don was boiling over with frustration, so more tobacco was distributed and Piet managed to coax the men outside. Natural curiosity overcame the women's initial reluctance, especially when they heard the men laughing, so at last, with their babies clutching tightly round their necks, they slowly swung down the pole, their movements disturbingly ape-like. As a reward for being first out of the hut, Don presented one of the women with a string of his bright blue glass beads. Nestling between her bosoms they glittered like sapphires; she looked almost regal.

Leaving Fane and Don to their photography, I went back inside the hut. Empty of its inhabitants it was a shell; surveying the litter, I felt like the last guest to leave a party. Out of the corner of my eye I caught a slight movement. Moving closer, I saw a young girl whom I had not noticed before. She was a pathetic sight, her beautiful features contorted with pain and her swollen arm suspended in a fibre sling from one of the overhead beams. Crude poultices of leaves and a sticky white substance covered the large puffy lumps on her thighs. As I raised my camera she turned away, moaning softly. I took the photograph but afterwards felt terrible remorse. Later I found out that she had been bitten by a snake.

Desperately needing fresh air, I crawled outside to find that Piet had been joined by a remarkable man. Two orang hutan, both holding long slender bows, accompanied him; they had just returned from a hunting trip in the jungle. His sophistication was in total contrast to the others. He was curiously dressed in an old pair of khaki shorts that hung to his knees, suspended by a highly polished Sam-Browne belt, which he caressed continually. He formally introduced himself, and shook each of us politely by the hand. This action seemed so incongruous to our surroundings that I found myself thinking we could be at a cocktail party and, at any moment, a white-coated waiter would appear, carrying a tray laden with glasses: 'Champagne, sir?' His name was Jumas, originally from Senggo, but for the last six years he had lived with this nomadic band as their leader, helping them in many ways, but particularly by sharing his skill as hunter and ace crocodile-catcher.

Possible subjects for photography had by now been exhausted and our tobacco supply was running dangerously low. Jumas was interested in our plans to push farther on up-river and immediately offered to accompany us as he knew the whereabouts of another encampment. He suggested taking an orang hutan to act as guide, and picked out a splendid individual who seemed entirely suitable for such an adventure. Two exceedingly long bone whiskers protruded vertically from his nostrils, resembling the waving antennae of a praying-mantis; from one ear swung a large hoop, fashioned from the quill of a cassowary feather; while below his rattan waistband hung the biggest pair of balls I had ever seen.

We wondered whether we should stay here and continue to photograph these people rather than push on immediately. We did not expect to be blessed with such fortune again. Jumas, however, assured us that we would be able to take more photographs on our return down-river, adding that they never moved far without him. His power over these people was incredible: his very presence drew them towards him as if they were hypnotised. He was almost like their god.

As we set off, I turned round expecting to see them lining the river banks, but they had already disappeared. I wondered what they had made of our visit. I felt a wave of enormous achievement, and I sensed Fane and Don felt the same.

I have often wondered what I would feel or say or do on coming face to face with such people. As a child I read many great epics of exploration which described such an event, and always longed for the moment when it would happen to me. And now that the moment itself had materialised, I remembered in detail my reaction on sticking my head into that dim and smoky interior. I can write no poignant description; I said and did and felt nothing; I simply stood and stared open-mouthed, just as they were staring at me.

★

I had never experienced such heat. The intense rays from the sun exploded and flashed on the metallic surface of the river: without our hats we would have been in trouble. Don's arms had turned a bright tomato red. Normally he would wear a long-sleeved shirt to protect them, but the extra layer of cloth had become intolerable and blisters bubbled ominously below the surface of his skin. Fane and I were wearing dark glasses and both suffering from severe headaches.

The river, too, had altered. The water itself was becoming increasingly clear; occasionally my eye was caught by a silver flash as a catfish slid by just below the surface. On the banks one could see the height to which the river rose in the rainy season, as it bullied and carved its way down from the mountains. Gone was the lush green vegetation which flourished on the banks of the rivers downstream; gone too the marvellously varied bird life which had enchanted and delighted us earlier. On the lower stretches we had disturbed thousands of birds, among them plump green pigeons, two-tone cockatoos, parrots in dazzling plumage. Now the only bird I saw was a sensible old heron cooling his feet in the shade of an overhanging palm. How I envied him.

As we progressed, our passage became increasingly difficult to navigate, demanding all of Joseph's and Alphonse's skills.

The river's depth was dropping rapidly and the water concealed enormous half-submerged trees. The current was unpredictable, and God alone knew what dangers lurked in the shadows of the banks. At intervals, Jumas would drop his arm to indicate that Joseph and Alphonse should cut the engines; we would then drift silently as he listened for sounds, standing motionless as a setter on point.

It was bloody uncomfortable and we became extremely irritable. Not even the memory of that morning or a cup of soup succeeded in cheering us up. Don again started to complain that Fane had obstructed his photography earlier on. As official photographer he was probably quite justified, as Fane and I did tend to fool around when we arrived somewhere, but this didn't help to sweeten our mood.

Rounding yet another narrow bend, we realised we must be approaching the source of the river and wondered how much farther we would be able to proceed by canoe. Small sandy spits were beginning to appear on both banks and we noticed Jumas shielding his eyes from the sun, carefully scanning them, though none of us knew why. Suddenly, with a loud grunt, he pointed excitedly to the nearest, causing us all to jump. What on earth had he seen? Forgetting the heat, we peered towards it – to me it looked no different from any other. The canoes were soon speeding towards the shore, and Jumas and the orang guide threw themselves off and rushed up the bank. Seizing two slender sticks, they began to probe the sand, first slowly and delicately, then more frantically, and soon they were scrabbling like dogs digging for bones. Intrigued and determined to get a closer look, we followed the example of our guides. Hurling ourselves from the canoe, we started to run up the sand. After two steps, we were back in the water, our feet smoking. They reappeared, carefully cradling something in their arms – two dozen turtle eggs, which in these parts are as exotic as caviar. It was uncanny how Jumas had managed to spot the turtle tracks from the canoe, and then locate the exact spot by following them across the beach.

Just a few minutes later we were again thrown into a flurry of activity. The canoe was carefully inching its way under a low-lying tree which jutted out from the bank, when our orang guide started furiously scratching his balls. He pointed a quivering finger at a huge crocodile stretched motionless on the bank before us. Its hide was a beautiful blend of dark and light tan; the tip of its tail dipped gracefully in the river, as one might dangle one's big toe. Fuck it, I thought. My first chance to bag a croc and I don't have the rifle. I gesticulated madly at Pak Polici, pointing at the bank. By the time he had manoeuvred himself into a firing position, the crocodile had swirled away into the depths.

'Deo!' I yelled. 'Tell him I want the gun!'

I could see Pak Polici shaking his head.

'He no want, *Harimau*. He frightened you shoot him!'

He was right.

Fifteen minutes later there was more excited scratching of balls and another smaller crocodile was spotted. This time the supply boat was ahead of us. I heard a dull crack and saw the tail twitch violently where the bullet had thudded home. It was a pathetic shot, considering the canoe was so close. Wounded, the crocodile dived and, before we knew what was happening, Jumas, the orang and Alphonse had followed. The water around them was whipped into a froth of pink bubbles as the crocodile's tail thrashed furiously from side to side. With a triumphant shout they finally grabbed it, while desperately avoiding the powerful jaws snapping at their legs. They yelled at us to bring a knife, but as usual 'Rambo' was safely tucked away in one of the bags. Unable to wait, the three men picked the crocodile up and started smashing its head against a tree stump, spattering us with flecks of blood.

As it was dragged from the water, the animal still seemed very much alive and, noticing Pak Polici eyeing it with concern, I told the boys to chuck it in the supply canoe.

Our headaches were now intolerable, and we were suffering from burning sensations in our cramped backsides and legs. To add to the torment we had run out of purified water, so that our tongues felt like sandpaper in our parched mouths. We also stank. The level of the river was so low that the rounded tops of boulders could now be seen: to my tired eyes each one resembled the back of a crocodile lurking below the surface. Then, with a sickening crunch of metal grinding against stone, the canoe came to an abrupt halt. Joseph was flung overboard, while the rest of us found ourselves entangled in a heap of limbs, tin boxes and oil drums, yelling abuse at one another. Stumbling to the stern, we found a bedraggled Joseph surveying the damaged engine through spirals of blue smoke. It seemed we had hit one of those underwater boulders, denting the cowling and completely shearing off one of the propeller blades. As the supply canoe arrived, a furious exchange flared up between Joseph and Deo. Deo yelled at Joseph, who yelled back, pushing him so that Deo fell over. Deo picked up a rock. Joseph brandished a spanner. Odd half-English, half-Indonesian insults were flung between them.

'*Rusak!*' (broken) Deo shouted. 'Fuckin' Jungle Johnnie. *Sama-sama Kera!*' (just like monkey).

'*Batak!*' Joseph growled, and spat on the ground.

We quickly intervened.

Ultimate responsibility for the accident lay with Joseph, who was supposed to be familiar with these rivers. He should probably have stopped earlier in order to protect our engine. He slunk away muttering under his breath. Personally, I appreciated his attempt to press on as far up-river as possible.

Wherever the blame lay, the jungle night was beginning to close in. We had to make a decision – either to leave the canoes here and continue on foot, or to turn back. I favoured the former plan, reckoning that we could stop here for the night and set off in the morning. Fane put the suggestion to Jumas, who conferred with the orang guide. It was not well received; neither of them was prepared to go any further. The people we were seeking were hostile, Jumas explained. By canoe we might have a chance, but on foot we would have no means of escape.

It was a hopeless situation. We knew that without our guides we were bound to get lost. We had already experienced Pak Polici's prowess with the rifle. Reluctantly, we conceded defeat and started downstream.

It seemed now that nothing could go right. Still sulking from being blamed for the accident and the insults which had been heaped on him, Joseph was not concentrating on navigation. Before long, we were racing past enormous boulders and narrowly missing tree stumps. Someone yelled a warning to him to 'turn sharp fucking left', and then we crashed headlong into a submerged tree. The impact of the sudden halt once again threw us around like puppets, while Fane, who had been sitting in the bows, was flung overboard into the swirling current. Soaking and considerably shaken, he just managed to grab the side of the canoe and we dragged him back on board.

We assessed the damage. Half the canoe was resting on the tree trunk, while the prow was wedged into the angle of a branch. We were taking on water rapidly. Joseph, anxious to redeem his credibility, plunged into the roaring water and was soon hacking away. None of us was anxious to join him. I looked around for the supply canoe, thinking it might tow us off, but it was already out of sight. There was no alternative. Gingerly clambering into the water, we fought against the current to join Joseph at the prow. Images of those powerful jaws tearing into our thighs lent us the strength born of sheer panic. With a final creak, the branch gave way and the canoe was free.

The supply canoe awaited us about a mile down-river. Judging by the murderous looks passing between Deo and Joseph, it would not be long before we had more trouble on our hands. Slowly we limped back, the vibrations caused by the broken propeller doing nothing to ease our discomfort and frayed tempers. By the time we reached the orang hutan encampment it was too dark to shoot any film. We dropped off Jumas and the guide, promising to return early next morning and continued on to Pattitipi. As we drew away from the shore I caught a gleam of vivid scarlet from high on the bank: the chief was already wearing his satin shorts.

We arrived at twilight, to be greeted by the now-familiar faces peering down at us from the bank. I was relieved to find that nobody was the worse for their diet of discarded film packets. We tumbled out into the cool water of the river and enjoyed a moonlit swim, bombarded by the bats.

Back in the hut, the pressure lamp had again packed up and Deo was making heavy work of plucking a chicken by candlelight. The boys had skinned the crocodile and were using parangs to hack off lumps of fatty meat, which were then dropped into a pot of boiling water. The chicken was my choice. While supper was cooking, we stumbled around in the darkness, attempting to hang our nets by the light of a weak torch. The mosquitoes were as ravenous as we were, and by the time we had finished we were sweaty, bitten and bloody-minded.

A bloated moon hung over the camp, bathing us in its jaundiced light. The night was humid and oppressive, a night conducive to violence and foul deeds.

The first culprit was Don. At last, Deo had put the finishing touches to the chicken and, with a flourish, proudly placed it before Fane and me. Considering the spartan facilities and lack of light, he had managed admirably: the chicken lay crisp and succulent and for a few tantalising moments we paused to inhale its delicious aroma. Don also eyed it with relish. The temptation was too great.

'Mmm, that looks good,' he remarked, and coolly tore off a leg.

Fane and I stared at him, stunned, and then with howls of indignation ripped it from his hand. During the ensuing argument, we required all our self-control to avoid coming to blows, and finished the meal in stony silence.

The second incident perhaps predictably involved the appalling boy, Zacchius. I was still shaking with rage after the Chicken Incident and wandered out the back to calm down in the fresh air. There I saw him, grinning insolently at me, a cigarette rakishly dangling from his petulant lip. Something warned me to look closer: it was one of *my* cigarettes. I was engulfed in icy, controlled anger; I wanted his blood!

Although short-tempered, I have experienced this particular feeling only once before in my life when, at the tender age of eight, I tried unsuccessfully to murder one of my sisters. I loathed her with an obsessive passion: she was everybody's favourite, she could do no wrong and when she did, I was blamed. In addition we were both extremely fat. That night, I whiled away the hours sharpening the little two-bladed pen-knife my father had given me for Christmas. At midnight, I wobbled naked along the moonlit passage to my sister's room, and slowly pushed open the door. She was lying on her bed like a giant blancmange, mouth wide open. I now had a choice. Either I could sneak forward and slip my knife into her belly while she snored, or I could wake her by launching myself with a shout, thus ensuring that her last sight on earth would be that of her demented brother and the glint of the descending weapon. That latter offered the more appropriate finale, so I leapt high into the air, whooping and slapping my backside like a Red Indian. Instantly I felt a sharp pain in my left buttock and, looking down, realised I had stabbed myself. My sister did not even wake up, and I spent the rest of the night sitting in the washbasin, where I was discovered the following morning, deathly pale from loss of blood. I had my explanation all prepared.

'I was playing with the knife in bed and must have sat on it.'

This was greeted with scepticism, but went unchallenged for some years, by which time I was very fond of my sister, whose shape had also improved with time.

Seeing the maddened look in my eyes, Zacchius backed away, flinching as I plucked the cigarette from his mouth. I picked up a parang, stained with crocodile blood, and advanced. He was saved by the Batak, who grabbed me from behind, snapping me back to reality.

Ashamed and emotionally exhausted, I went quietly to bed.

CHAPTER NINE

Cannibals

A good night's sleep had dispelled our irascibility, and spirits were high as we left early for the orang hutan dwelling. We took the supply canoe, piloted by Alphonse, leaving Joseph to apply his mechanical genius to the broken engine. I noticed that Zacchius stayed behind as well.

We arrived to find that Jumas and most of the men had set off early to hunt pig. Photographically, it was almost better half-deserted, particularly when Piet negotiated for one side of the hut to be removed. Sunlight flooded in, illuminating the occupants: most of the women and children were there, including the sick girl I had photographed the previous day. I cleaned and bandaged her swollen arm and legs as best I could, but she was still in terrible pain. When I produced an aspirin, the women who seemed to be looking after her became extremely suspicious. They peered and sniffed at the little white pill; one woman tasted it and spat in disgust. Ultimately we knew that the girl would heal or die regardless of our efforts, but my concern had promoted a feeling of trust, and the atmosphere was friendly.

I wanted to know how the rattan armband was used to make fire. One of the remaining men was wearing one and seemed to understand when I pointed to it. First he bound together two dry sticks, which held some dried moss sandwiched between them. Next, he uncoiled the length of rattan from his arm and passed it beneath the sticks, which he held firmly with his feet. Then he rapidly drew the rattan up and down under the sticks, the friction gradually generating heat, and eventually sparking the tinder.

After this display of ingenuity, I thought it might be presumptuous if I were to offer to use my lighter to light the pipes which they were now starting to prepare. The tobacco was rolled tightly in a long leaf, resembling a thin panatella cigar, and then the tip was placed in one end of a bamboo tube, which was beautifully incised with strange abstract designs. One end of the tube had already been filled with grass, presumably to form a kind of filter. The 'cigar' was then held above the flame and, with a deep inhalation, the smoke drawn through the tube. I held out my hand and they watched wide-eyed as I took an enormous drag, immediately dissolving into an uncontrolled fit of coughing, tears streaming from my eyes. My audience roared with laughter, rocking backwards and forwards on their heels.

I was not the only one to provide entertainment. Don was clambering around the hut, camera snapping busily, when suddenly the floor collapsed and he disappeared. We rushed to the gaping hole, fearing all kinds of terrible injury, only to see him dusting himself down and cursing eloquently. These war photographers are a tough breed.

The orang hutan proudly displayed Jumas's crocodile-catcher, which was lying along the bamboo rafters. This ingenious implement comprised a long thick bamboo pole with a noose at one end. This was made from a tough fibre and weighted with small stones, and could be adjusted like a slipknot. Hunting took place by canoe at night when crocodiles were asleep on the river banks. When the hunters spotted a suitable victim they glided silently towards it and slowly manoeuvred the noose over the tail. Often there were casualties in the ensuing pandemonium as they wrestled with the beasts. It sounded a splendid sport.

It was time to go. Not only had Don exhausted his supply of film, but we were being plagued by a swarm of black sticky flies (known locally as pig flies) which did not bite, but rather crawled into every orifice of one's body. We left some parting gifts: as much tobacco as we could spare, some salt and a mirror, which caused considerable excitement. This time, they

seemed sorry to see us go, lining the banks to watch our
departure. My last memory of them was of one man peering
intently into the mirror and stroking his grey beard. He
reminded me of Don who, when not hunched over a camera,
spent most of his time glued to a mirror, checking the progress
of his beard.

Back at Pattitipi we found our companions sprawled fast
asleep in the canoe. Later, juddering downstream, it was clear
that Joseph's mechanical morning had been a waste of time: the
vibrations were even more violent than before, inspiring Fane
to name our canoe the *Dildo*.

We stopped several times on the way to photograph and trade
with passing canoes. One man would have escaped our notice
had it not been for a sudden flash of silver against the green
background: he was holding aloft a gleaming catfish. His canoe
was nestling among the overhanging foliage and as we
approached we could see it contained his family – a woman,
three children and two dogs. The man himself was tall and
powerfully built, not afflicted by any skin disease, though his
testicles were somewhat enlarged. We were not desperate for
the fish or the bow and arrow which he offered us, but he was so
cheerful that we took them anyway in exchange for a sizeable
wad of tobacco. Scratching his balls vigorously, he dived into
the bottom of his canoe and produced an enormous bunch of
unripe bananas, which we accepted gratefully. It was only in
retrospect that we realised we had robbed him of everything he
owned, although he had seemed delighted with the transaction.

We stopped to trade again at a village farther down-river,
where our booty consisted of a stone axe, a small shield, and a
rather exotic G-string made from cassowary feathers, which
Fane procured. I presumed it would be a gift for his wife, but I
could not help thinking it would be more suitable around the
gyrating pelvis of a Bangkok bar girl than in Sloane Square.

High on the banks, we saw many huts, apparently deserted.
At the entrance of one stood an old man carrying something
black and huge between his legs. It looked like a coal sack.

Drawing closer we realised that he was suffering from an advanced state of elephantiasis: the coal sack turned out to be his scrotum which hung down below his knees. Considering this excellent material for my forthcoming 'Private Parts' exhibition, I swiftly fixed on my long lens, but my subject lumbered inside his hut, where he stayed, resolutely ignoring even the lure of tobacco. Don and Fane looked at me with disgust.

The day dragged interminably, our discomfort growing more acute with every minute. It was a great relief when we finally reached the confluence of the rivers and turned off the Brassa on to the Sirets, which would take us to Mbinamzein, the day's destination. By six o'clock we were exhausted, drenched with sweat and spray, and suffering agonies from squatting all day on those loathsome tin boxes. I had spent a full hour racking my brains to remember whether my doctor had included medication for piles in my kit, and wondering what natural remedies I could try if he hadn't.

In the last moments of daylight we pulled into Mbinamzein. At first the village appeared deserted – no firelight or smoke, no voices. As we approached the bank dark shapes began to materialise from nowhere. They must have heard the uneven splutter of our engines. Dazzling white teeth flashed in what we could only hope were welcoming smiles, and the whites of their eyes gleamed as they peered into the dark canoes in anticipation.

Ignoring the shooting pains in my back and legs, I clambered ashore and squinted into the gloom to gain some impression of our surroundings. Outlined against the darkening sky I made out several very tall trees standing away from any others and balancing in their topmost branches some kind of structure. At that distance they resembled rooks' nests; coming closer, I saw they were tiny tree-houses, perched precariously at least 100 feet above the ground. I beckoned to Joseph, hoping he could explain their significance. These, he told me, were used both as look-out posts and fortresses during the frequent wars between villages. From their high vantage point, the villagers could spot the approach of invaders and prepare to attack. If the enemies attempted to fell the tree, a flurry of arrows would rain down, and the wood was usually too damp to burn effectively.

Back at the river, Piet was organising the unloading, barking out orders and distributing tobacco. Our provisions and kitbags were soon snaking their way on the backs of the villagers up the muddy path to our accommodation for the night, supervised along this part of the route by the watchful Batak.

Following behind, we found ourselves on the front porch of a large timber house. It belonged to a Dutch missionary who had gone away for a few months. Piet forced open the door and we tumbled in. The interior was spacious and clean and was even equipped with a tap providing running water. This was a rare treat. Not for us tonight the stink of rotting rattan floorboards and a roof open to the elements. We checked out the rooms, Fane, Don and I picking our absent host's own bedroom for our lodging. To guard us during the night, we decided that Deo and Piet should sleep outside our door. We were taking no chances. Returning outside, we found that Deo and Alphonse, our resident botanists, had picked all the lilies which the missionary had lovingly cultivated by his front porch.

We couldn't stand the smell of each other any longer, and immediately took advantage of the magnificent bathing facilities offered by our absent host. In Indonesia, the correct method of washing is to scoop the water from whatever receptacle is provided and then douse one's body. On seeing the six huge oil drums brimming with fresh rainwater, we simply climbed in.

Deo had conjured up some food and carefully placed the dishes in front of each of us: sardines and rice for Fane and me, a silver package for Don. We were impressed by his tact. The boys were chewing on the remains of the boiled crocodile, while Zacchius gnawed contentedly on a raw piece of its head. We could hear frantic scrabbling around the house when the remains were flung outside.

After dinner we sat around fiddling with my radio, but received poor reception. Hearing the news flashes of air disasters and freezing August weather at home, we smirked to ourselves and decided we were infinitely better off here. Meanwhile, Joseph was planning more traditional entertainment. Popping the last gristly morsel of crocodile into his cavernous mouth, and wiping his hands on one of my clean sarongs, he fixed us with a stare which the Ancient Mariner might have envied and began his tales of the notorious Kolff River. Spreading the map on the floor in front of us, he traced our route with an oil-stained finger. Our first stop would be the *kampong* (village) of Samosir. Then we would continue a couple of hours further up-river to Wortu, where we might spend the night, depending on how the villagers reacted to our arrival. A short distance from there was an area inhabited by the notoriously fierce Butu tribe, which zealously refuses contact with all outsiders. The last (living) person to have seen them was a villager travelling down a small tributary of the Kolff. Only last year, according to Joseph, the headman of Mbinamzein met a gory end. He was savagely hacked to pieces, and his remains were found in the jungle, near Wortu. Also, several years before, a nasty incident befell some geologists sent to the area by an American oil company. During the night they were suddenly attacked. One of the geologists was wounded and they were lucky to escape with their lives.

The resourceful Joseph had already devised a scheme in case the Butu's response to our arrival was hostile. We would take just one canoe and slowly ease our way up the tributary (backwards, Don sensibly suggested, in order to avoid the frightful business of turning round). On reaching a certain spot, Joseph would leave some tobacco on the ground. We would then wait. If the Butu took the tobacco it meant we might be welcome; if it was left untouched—assuming they were in the area—we should get out of there fast.

Joseph sat back, delighted with his scheme, but we doubted his ability to start the engine in a moment of crisis. However, it seemed ridiculous to contemplate defeat, so what the hell?

Our imaginations filled with gruesome images, we crawled under our nets and tried to sleep. About half an hour later I awoke from a state of semi-consciousness aware of something scuttling around by my left ear. Heart pounding, I grabbed the torch and directed the beam at a spider as large as a soup plate. I shot out of my bed, yelling for the trusty Batak. After a wild chase, during which everybody's sleeping arrangements were overturned, Don appeared from under my mat triumphantly brandishing the beast on the end of a parang. Feeling sheepish, I retired again to my bed. My behaviour did not make a good impression on the others, but I noticed they secured their mosquito nets with special care, and I could swear I heard 'Rambo' being drawn from its sheath.

★

Our early departure was delayed by the obstinate outboard on the main canoe. We shifted from foot to foot in the pouring rain, as Joseph again applied his uniquely Indonesian skills to the problem. To the casual observer it seemed that the moment the engine refused to start Joseph would whip off the casing and, muttering under his breath, beat it soundly with his rusty hammer. I suspected there could be more to it than met the eye; that morning the spirits were on his side, for after only a couple of thumps it hiccoughed into life and we gingerly lowered our sore arses on to the tin boxes. We were accompanied by a local boy from Mbinamzein who was familiar with the area and whose presence offered a certain protection to the rest of us. He sat huddled in the prow looking miserable and alarmed, perhaps regretting his decision to join us in exchange for a yellow T-shirt. I hoped it was true that there was safety in numbers.

The rain ceased as suddenly as it had begun and now the sky was leaden and overcast; the oppressive humidity induced a feeling of lethargy and uneasiness. Conversation was kept to a minimum as the three of us sat slumped in the canoe, dozing fitfully.

22 Arriving at Wortu, in the heart of cannibal country

23 Trouble begins with the approach of Chief Abu

24 *Left*, the closer he came the more formidable he looked

26 *Opposite left*, food for a hungry crew: Shand and Fane display the crocodile

27 *Opposite right*, Alphonse and cassowary – the bird deserved more respectful treatment

28 *Opposite below*, the canoes being loaded with orchids at Woowi

25 *Below*, several of the men moved silently to squat on the prow

29 Family out on the Forets River

30 American Express – don't leave home without it!

During my periods of consciousness, I sensed something very sinister about the Kolff River; I was convinced that we were being followed and observed. I became particularly uneasy when the canoe was forced nearer the banks to negotiate a safe passage through the swirling currents. This river was much narrower than the Brassa, and the currents more powerful. The *Dildo* was feeling the strain, shaking and juddering so much that when we spoke we developed terrible stutters. There was noticeably little bird life. Perched like a sentry, the occasional eagle glared at us with furious yellow eyes.

We reached the village of Samosir in two hours. As we nosed the canoes towards the bank, Joseph called into the jungle, but his words were absorbed into the silence which hung like a shroud of mist over the river. It was completely deserted: only a couple of huts were left standing, and partially submerged in the mud were two rotting canoes. It was a sad place with a sense of lurking evil, and I was relieved when we moved on. I found out later that it had been ravaged by an epidemic which had swept through the area recently, leaving many villages abandoned.

After a time, we spotted a man in a small canoe, standing as motionless as a heron. Against the bright green undergrowth we could just make out that he was holding aloft a bunch of bananas. We already had far too many, so we waved lazily and pressed on up-river.

We were all restless now, itching to stretch our legs. The heat was unbearable and the tin boxes became too hot to sit on. At last we reached Wortu. While we were tying up the canoes, a number of villagers appeared, giggling or glaring, depending on their sex. This was Zacchius's home, so we instructed him to ask if they had anything to trade, secretly hoping a few skulls might be forthcoming. A quick sift through revealed nothing but bones, bows and arrows, and the odd spear. We asked Zacchius to inquire specifically, but quickly dropped the subject when we saw the terror on his face. As a gesture of courtesy Piet distributed salt, fishing line and tobacco. Don had wandered off and was arranging people in photogenic groups. Fane and I carefully kept out of the way and sprawled in the shade, smoking fags.

The men were a mean bunch, like primitive football hooligans. They suffered from the usual skin disease, which we had now discovered was called 'Frambrosia'. It sounded deceptively like a delicious cocktail, but in fact was caused by vitamin deficiency. In common with the other people we had met in this area, the villagers had the most disconcerting habit of constantly turning their heads from side to side, as if trying to minimise contact with us. I can't say I blamed them: to them we must have appeared monstrous.

We were relieved to learn that the fearsome Butu people had left the area a month ago to find new hunting ground. We decided to continue up the Kolff River, hoping eventually to make contact with a tribe of 'tree-people'. Collecting the equipment, we reassembled on the river bank. I noticed that one ingenious man had attached an empty plastic film canister to the tip of his penis and was exhibiting his acquisition to the others. As we prepared to board the canoes, we realised that while we were in the village, Joseph had completely dismantled the *Dildo*'s engine and was in the throes of one of his incantations. Nuts, bolts and strands of coloured wire strewed the canvas like confetti. We were obliged to resign ourselves to yet another wait and sat around frying like eggs in the scorching sun. Meanwhile, the men had arranged themselves in a neat semi-circle around us, fidgeting with their weapons and making us nervous with their odd jerky movements.

A canoe drew up on the far side of the supply boat in which Deo, Alphonse and Pak Polici were waiting. It did not bother us until Fane realised that it contained the same man who had offered us bananas on the way into the village, and who was now identified as the *Kepala Perang*. For a few tense moments the only sounds were the thumps of Joseph's hammer and the low murmur of conversation between Zacchius and the chief. Quite suddenly, he shouted and started gesticulating in an alarming manner, growing increasingly agitated. The atmosphere became menacing. He was one of the least prepossessing individuals I have ever seen. He was tall and still strong, his grey beard framing the mouth of a shark, crowded with strong yellow teeth.

Even the less acute members of our crew had by now realised that we were the cause of his rage and that it would be expedient to leave. We moved to the canoe, climbed in and sat waiting. The entire crew had lapsed into nervous silence; Pak Polici stared at his feet. Why the hell didn't he get the gun?

'They're surrounding us,' whispered Fane, noticing that several of the men had moved silently from the bank to squat on the prow directly behind Don. A few seconds later, the chief climbed out of his canoe and perched on the side close to Deo. Usually the very picture of happiness, the Batak went completely to pieces: his face turned grey, sweat poured off him and he started hyperventilating.

The only member of the crew to behave sensibly was Piet, who carried on distributing tobacco. We sat there grinning, calculating the odds on it running out before the engine was fixed. Fane, his hands hidden by the side of the canoe, fumbled for the reassuring shape of 'Rambo'.

'For God's sake, don't light a fag and don't try taking a photograph,' Fane hissed at me.

'I don't know about you, but I'm going to swim for it,' Don breathed into my ear.

The *Kepala Perang* screamed suddenly. I saw a bow being drawn. At the same moment the engine roared into life. Deo grabbed the Mauser and waved it in the air, a sight which surprised the chief so much that he toppled over backwards. Seizing his chance, the Batak rushed to the front, untied the rope and yelled at Alphonse to get moving. Quick as an arrow the canoe shot away and whizzed downstream. Joseph opened the throttle and attempted to follow. We were stuck in the mud! Piet grabbed an entire box of tobacco and flung it on to the bank. Don and I hurled ourselves over the prow, knocked the tribesmen off the side, and with an almighty shove launched the canoe into the safety of the river.

As we were swept away with the current, we were overcome with euphoria, laughing hysterically and hurling abuse at our enemies. Within half a mile we caught up with the other canoe and, drawing alongside, headed downstream, shouting over the reassuring splutter of the engines.

We did not realise how lucky we had been until Deo extracted the full story from our guide. The War Chief, whose name was Abu, had achieved a certain notoriety in the area: no fewer than eight people in the last four years have been his victims. We had offended him on three accounts: first, we did not stop to talk to him on the river; next, we had spurned his bananas; finally, we had neglected to request his permission to enter the village.

In addition our guide related to us a conversation he had overheard between the chief and his warriors. Abu had told them that when they attacked they should be sure to kill the 'long one' first. In retrospect, I remembered the chief casting furtive glances at Fane's legs, which were draped elegantly over the side of the canoe. Though he has always had a 'good leg for a boot', Fane was not flattered.

The threat to Deo's life was far graver than we had realised. From our position we had been unable to see that one of Abu's henchmen, hidden by the bulk of the Batak's body, was holding a drawn arrow directly at the base of his spine.

We continued down-river with some difficulty, attempting to hold the canoes together as yet again our engine had seized up and we were unwilling to stop before we had put as much distance as possible between ourselves and Abu. Joseph wanted to spend another night at Mbinamzein in order to fix the engine, but we were keen to leave the Kolff altogether. We imagined the ease with which Abu and his gang could paddle downstream in the blackness of night, flick aside our mosquito nets and slaughter us in our sleep. Our crew persuaded us that this could not occur, sarcastically pointing out our fortune in having Pak Polici to protect us.

Further excitement lay in store for us. During a torrential downpour we were huddled like wet dogs in the bottom of the canoe, when I happened to peer over the side. I immediately spotted a large crocodile, at least eight feet long, lying on a log about forty yards away. Its colouring blended so well with its surroundings that it could easily have escaped my notice. We were directly alongside and I did not intend to miss *this* opportunity.

'Pak Polici,' I whispered furiously. *'Buaya besar* (big crocodile). Give me the gun.'

He refused.

I lunged across into the supply boat, but my movement forced the canoes apart. We were now too close to the crocodile. Hearing the engine, it slid off the log. Pak Polici's bloody-minded behaviour almost caused a mutiny. I had never seen the boys so angry: they were for dropping him overboard, and it was with some reluctance that the rest of us intervened. The crocodile would have provided numerous meals for the crew – who, I was sure, would run out of their own food before long and start 'borrowing' our meagre rations.

Exhausted, we stumbled into the hut in Mbinamzein. The boys built up a roaring fire and after supper we gathered together in the warmth. The extraordinary events of the day fuelled a lively discussion. Looking round at the animated faces, I realised why I was feeling especially content: Zacchius was no longer with us. In the general excitement I had failed to notice that he had stayed at Wortu. Good riddance! We were back to our original team again and linked even closer by the bond of shared danger. For the first time I realised that I had become fond of our motley crew.

CHAPTER TEN

Words of Warning

After the excitement of the last few days we felt numb and deflated. Besides a sense of anticlimax, we were burdened with the problem of a broken engine, which curtailed any immediate plans to explore new territory. We sat around outside while Joseph attempted to coax the outboard back to life. From time to time the still morning air would be shattered by the rasp of the stuttering engine, and ugly gouts of oily black smoke would rise in coils above the scrub on the river bank. Eventually, Joseph appeared, scowling and covered with grease stains, to announce that the engine was dead. As a temporary measure, he suggested roping the canoes together at prow and stern, the occupants of each canoe joining hands to prevent the sides colliding.

Forcing ourselves to shake off our lethargy, we decided to head directly down-river to Woowi, to collect our extra fuel and assess the options.

Villagers were pressganged into acting as porters, and soon the colourful procession was snaking back down to the river. The canoes were roped together and loaded, presenting a bizarre sight, closely resembling that of a funeral flotilla of some oriental potentate. An assortment of ancient weaponry – bows and arrows, stone axes, spears and shields – all but filled the supply vessel, which was barely visible beneath a dazzling array of huge orchid plants which Deo had collected along the way. I failed to spot the crocodile skin. Tethered by blue plastic string to the prow of the *Dildo* were four extra passengers – a black cockerel and three hens. Pak Polici had engaged in some useful trading the night before.

Like lovers embarking on some fiendish ride at an amusement park, we lurched into midstream, tightly clutching hands. We felt extremely foolish, and it soon became clear that the plan was a failure. Despite Joseph's assurances to the contrary, it was impossible to hold the boats tightly alongside without the sides slamming together. Each time this happened the edges painfully pinched our forearms and we were soaked by the spouts of water which were forced through the gap.

Pretty soon I tired of Indonesian ways and, demanding an immediate halt, suggested an alternative: we would transfer the engine to the *Dildo* and proceed in tandem, towing the supply canoe. This horrified the Indonesian sector, particularly the Batak, who for some obscure reason now considered himself a nautical expert. They insisted that it would swing uncontrollably and overturn.

Deaf to their pleas, we demanded instant execution of my orders, and they grudgingly complied, in the process almost dropping the working engine in the river. A dramatic lurch and terrified cries from Deo accompanied our departure, but once the tow rope was sufficiently taut my plan worked beautifully. I stuck a derisive finger in their direction.

The dullness of the journey was broken only by a short stop at a village that seemed familiar. When a struggling cassowary joined the rest of the cargo, I realised this was the place to which we had delivered that same bird. It belonged to Alphonse, who had deposited it here for safe-keeping while we were up-river. I was glad to see it still alive and kicking.

We chugged on, bodies, heads and engines throbbing. The sky cleared and we stripped off our clothes, basking in the hot sun and hoping to touch up our fading tans. I spread-eagled myself on the prow and was beginning to relax when one of the hens shook out her plumage and plumped down on my stomach, where she went to sleep.

It was late afternoon by the time we arrived at Woowi, a friendly village set well back from the river. To reach the schoolhouse, we had to cross a large waterlogged meadow; a line of logs acted as a causeway. There must have been heavy rain recently, for when I stepped on to the first log, it slipped from under my feet and floated away. It was much simpler to wade or swim. The schoolhouse was clean and airy. A blackboard dominated one end of the room; we set up camp at the other, draping our nets over the desks.

The missionaries had kept their word: four 44-gallon drums awaited us. Now we were faced with a serious weight problem: full drums would put a severe strain on the small outboard engine which had already exceeded expectation in transporting us here. Either we would have to rely on Joseph to accomplish a massive repair job, or find another engine to replace the broken one. Both seemed equally unlikely, but with everything to lose, we dispatched Alphonse and Deo to Senggo to see what they could organise.

We found ourselves arguing with Piet about whose responsibility it was to pay for a new outboard. He pleaded that Manu would be angry about the damaged engine and would probably offset the cost of a new one by refusing to pay the crew. Remembering the tough negotiation back in Merauke, this seemed likely, so reluctantly we agreed to split the cost.

Bored with machines and money, I waded out into the meadow and sat down on a wet log, with a view over the river. The evening was perfectly still. Canoes glided past, hardly causing a ripple to disturb the millpond calm of the water; flies buzzed drowsily and a pigeon cooed somewhere in the jungle on the far bank. Beside me, on a branch drooping low over the water, perched a kingfisher, its beady eyes watching the tiny fish skimming below the surface. Its lustrous markings were distinct and seemed to combine all the colours of the rainbow in dazzling contrast – an orange breast, iridescent blue wings, a blood-red head. Like a raindrop, it suddenly fell from the branch, hardly denting the surface, but missed the prey and returned to its perch, shaking the moisture from its feathers. I sat there for a long time; it was a relief to be alone. I waited until the sun dipped below the jungle line and then slowly headed back across the meadow, so lost in thought that I barely noticed Don, who was on his way down, clutching a bar of soap.

A few villagers had gathered at the schoolhouse. One of them offered me a fine dagger made of cassowary bone. I was tempted but, remembering my trussed friend, declined. Another villager, wearing an old cane hat, was propped against the white clapboard, tunelessly strumming a crudely made guitar with only one string. Listening to the monotonous 'plonk', I was struck by the incongruous situation: I could have been holidaying in the Caribbean rather than in a remote jungle thousands of miles from anywhere.

I went indoors to bring my diary up to date. Sitting at a desk, gazing aimlessly at the blackboard, I was transported back in time and could almost imagine the scowling schoolmaster and the painfully accurate sting of a piece of chalk. 'Shand! Pay attention, you lazy little blighter!' . . .

Later, above the hiss of the pressure lamp, we could hear the thumps and crashes and curses as Joseph worked at the engine outside. We sat in the dark, listening in silence as Piet recounted a strange event which had happened a few years ago when he was working for an Indonesian timber company. The main camp was set up near the river – the Brassa – and he was sent with a local guide to find and mark suitable trees for felling. Without warning, they found themselves surrounded by a large group of orang hutan, including women and children. They were heavily armed and brandished drawn bows. The chief was in a towering rage, claiming that Piet was in violation of his territory, and demanded obeisance. Piet was forced to crawl between the legs of ten of the chief's wives and then suck the milk from their breasts. Resistance would have meant instant death. Relating the tale his face, illuminated in the glow of our cigarettes, gleamed ashen white, as though the memory of this experience was making him physically ill. It appeared that we had escaped lightly from our encounter with Abu. I remembered only too clearly the rank smell and diseased bodies of the women we had encountered.

When he had recovered his composure, I asked Piet about their sexual habits. His knowledge was limited to what he had been told by the local people, who said that mating took place in a clearing in the jungle when the moon was full. The man would position his wives on all fours and then deal with them one after another in rapid succession.

'Not like me: I like jig-a-jig *pelan-pelan!*' (slowly, slowly) Piet added with a grin.

He was better informed about the habits of the Asmatters, the people from the coastal area we hoped to explore next. Until very recently, it appeared, they would indulge in huge orgies, lasting for days. They gathered together in a pool of water or shallow river, and copulated in a maddened frenzy. They then drank the semen and blood-filled water, believing it invested them with strength and power. The missionaries had worked to put an end to this practice, as many Asmatters had contracted deadly diseases.

Piet also told us about another incident which had occurred the year before in a village close to where we would be going. A frenzied mass killing had taken place. Many people were slaughtered and women and childen raped. When the police arrived, they found only the skulls and bones of people who had died naturally. On further investigation they were led to a spot where they dug up fresh remains. Four or five men were, in Piet's words, 'put in a big steel box'. They were locked up in Agats for a few months and then released.

The authorities are powerless against such things, which happen frequently and are the way of the country. Piet warned us that although the Asmatters may be more civilised than the jungle people we had met, we should not be deceived by appearances. They may *seem* friendly, he said, but underneath the T-shirts and the veneer of sophistication they are potentially very dangerous. We didn't sleep too well that night.

CHAPTER ELEVEN

The Casuarina Coast

Deo returned from his trip to Senggo with bad news: there was no suitable engine available. Nevertheless, he had managed to retrieve our *Surat Jalan* from the policeman without money changing hands.

'Mrs Polis, Ibu Augustine, hot for Fane, so I no pay nothing,' Deo whispered, nudging me in the conspiratorial manner of a tout offering dirty postcards. He also brought a package for me, accompanied by a note from the missionaries explaining its contents (see overleaf).

The remedy had arrived too late – my problem had been solved by the meeting with Chief Abu.

After several attempts, the heavy petrol drums were heaved into the bellies of the canoes – a hot, frustrating process, requiring help from the villagers and some well-placed logs. It was a remarkable achievement, considering that contradictory orders were being issued in both English and Indonesian. Joseph attached to the stern a Heath Robinson contraption that was held together by lengths of nylon fishing line. It was the damaged outboard. We listened in silence as, with a wheezy choke, it spluttered into life. Its irregular running was worrying, but at least it gave us a chance of reaching our next destination, Atsj.

We set off, again in tandem, but now with the larger engine taking the strain of the heavy load. The heat grew more intense by the minute and progress was painfully slow. At intervals the engine mysteriously died, and we would drift down-river while Joseph carried out running repairs. Sometimes, both engines

Pastoran 21-8

Hi,

These suppositories are only meant against-colic - if you have severe pains. The juice of one or 2 fresh coconuts : the soft flesh of a young COCONUT should also expedite matters, to SLOWLY DRIVE THE CONTENTS FORWARD.
Black coffee may help : tea does not stimulate the peristaltic movement.
A horse-medicine : warm a small piece of SOAP and shove it up where it should be : that should expedite matters ! TRY
Sorry, we have no direct medicine to influence the bowels.
Drink plenty of boiled water !

Yours Bon.

P.S. Do keep the bowels open.

The missionaries provide a remedy

gave up the ghost simultaneously. While Joseph and Alphonse tinkered with them, we were embarrassed to be overtaken by the canoes we had imperiously chugged past earlier. The occupants, wielding their paddles, laughed at our plight. Our own efficient crew had neglected to supply such humble implements – well, why on earth would *we* need them?

During this journey we all engaged in different activities to alleviate the boredom. Fane dozed, Don cast his fishing line, and I was so hot that I would dive into the river to cool off. My face had been lacerated by the fierce sun and now resembled a partly peeled peach. Strips of skin like old yellow Sellotape hung from my nose and cheekbones. Unfortunately, my straw hat failed to offer much protection. It had seen better days and the fraying edges were ineffectively held together by Elastoplast. Our unfortunate livestock were also suffering. Tethered to the prow the hens were visibly wilting in the heat and, judging by their appearance, an oven would soon be unnecessary. The cockerel, on the other hand, was thriving. It seemed to have been driven into a sexual frenzy, relentlessly pecking at the backs of the hens' necks, leaving them bald and bleeding. Amorous advances these may have been, but such sadistic behaviour was not a pleasing spectacle. I quickly put an end to it by viciously tweaking a handful of glossy feathers from its backside.

My friend, the cassowary, was not faring much better. At regular intervals Alphonse would startle it by unceremoniously grabbing the long neck and dunking its head over the side of the canoe. This enforced cooling off seemed a grossly unfair and humiliating experience for such a splendid bird. Considering it would probably be made into feathered G-strings long before the end of its brief natural lifespan, I felt it deserved more respectful treatment.

Often when I'm bored I find myself singing the opening bars of a song, then repeating them over and over, quite unable to get rid of them, for hours on end. Early that morning there the tune was, firmly attached. I imagined the words sung by Lee

Marvin, in a gravelly, saloon-type voice: '*Whisky and gin, whisky and gin . . .*' This mindless repetition drove Don and Fane into apoplectic rages, but their begging me to stop merely fuelled my desire to sing. It seemed to harmonise nicely with the sound of the engines. I knew that whenever I repeated those magic words in the future I would be transported back to the canoe, would see the blinding shimmer of the river, feel the discomfort of the tin box welded to my backside, and hear Joseph's curses as he hammered at the engine.

It was a sad moment when we forked left on to the Betsj River, leaving the Sirets behind – like taking leave of an old and faithful friend. The jungle began to thin out, gradually becoming marshy, and we saw ducks and geese. We were approaching the sea: I could smell it. A tiny houseboat floated past, puffing smoke from its roof like a runaway miniature train. It was completely empty.

How easy it is to wax lyrical about sunsets, but that evening's was very special. Each tree, each leaf and each cloud was reflected in perfect detail on the glassy surface of the river. The great golden orb descended majestically, turning to a deep purple the metallic mass of storm clouds rapidly building up behind us, swelling until they looked like huge ripe plums. The dramatic magnificence seemed to me a suitable valediction to our days upstream.

Gradually the river widened into an estuary, and there in the twilight we were shocked to see a myriad twinkling lights: Atsj. This was scarcely 'civilisation' – most of the lights were simply small fires and kerosene lamps – but we would have preferred a more gradual return. After ten days of such isolation we felt bewildered and disorientated.

We moored outside a shack the colour of vomit, which reverberated to the plangent screeching of electric guitars. Inside, two unsavoury youths clad in T-shirts and tight jeans were sprawled near a cassette-player attached to an old car battery. Their heads jerked up and down to the rhythm: the 1960s had finally arrived in Atsj. The walls were fashionably plastered with gory film posters depicting voluptuous doe-eyed women vainly clutching ripped blouses to their exposed bosoms, while strange *samurai*-like warriors stood astride them, brandishing enormous curved swords and snarling. One wall was dedicated to a full-length colour poster of Gary Glitter, who bulged from a skin-tight sequinned outfit while managing to look curiously disapproving. Perhaps it was due to the small Hitler moustache someone had pencilled in on his top lip.

This delightful residence was the local 'rest house'. We were informed that we could pay 50,000 rupiah (forty-five dollars) for the pleasure of staying. Joseph was in his element, changing the cassettes and yelling, '*Bagus, bagus* (good, good), eh? *Deesco, deesco?*' Over our dead bodies. Disdain written all over our faces, we fixed the riverside rockers with withering glares and marched out, slamming the door.

Piet disappeared to find alternative accommodation, soon returning like the Pied Piper, followed by a crowd of small boys. He explained that they were orphans and were in the process of building – by themselves – an orphanage. Their faces lit up when Fane asked if we might stay the night with them. They insisted on carrying our heaviest bags, and were soon struggling along under their loads, leaving us to follow. It was pitch dark, and we had to cross a deep canal, the hull of a slim upturned canoe acting as a makeshift bridge. It looked dangerously slippery. Seeing our hesitation, the boys clambered nimbly across with the luggage, then returned to lead each of us over, taking us by the hand as one would guide a blind man over the road.

Half the orphanage still lacked a roof. The boys insisted we use the covered part and helped set up mosquito nets and inflate Lilos. The Batak was enjoying himself immensely: the children adored him and crowded round like bees to a honey pot. This seemed an appropriate place to celebrate our safe return from the wilds. Deo was sent to find beer. There was none available (I don't know why we imagined there would be), but he returned laden with packets of sticky sweets for the children.

Later we all drew close to a blazing fire, sharing our food. I watched the expressions on their eager faces turn from astonishment to delight as the Batak kept them spellbound with tales of our perilous adventures. I knew I would recall that evening with pleasure when, back in London, I found myself enduring trivial conversation at some dull dinner party.

I was woken at dawn by the ghastly wailing of the muezzin calling his people to morning prayer, and lay thanking God I was not a Moslem. Having to rise so early every day would be a nightmare.

We planned to reach Jou, a village near the sea, by evening. The next few days would be spent exploring the romantic-sounding Casuarina coast. The Casuarina tree (incidentally, the title of a collection of stories by Somerset Maugham) is a species of beef-wood found mainly in Australia and this part of the world, so named because of its resemblance to the plumage of the cassowary bird, which we had been able to study at close quarters the previous day. We intended to stop at various settlements in the vicinity, primarily to engage in some serious and, we hoped, lucrative trading.

Yet again we were to fall foul of the vagaries of both man and machine. Our faithful old engine was now useless. The journey would include long stretches of open sea, and the fate of Michael Rockefeller served as a warning to us. Piet and Joseph set off to find a replacement. We didn't trust them, so we sent the Batak in the opposite direction to see what he could ferret out. Our doubts seemed justified when, far too quickly, the former arrived back, beaming, and announced that an engine was available for only 15,000 rupiah (twelve dollars) per day. Certain they had struck a side-deal with the riverside rockers, we beamed back woodenly. Deo then reappeared, having managed to locate a similar engine for *10,000* per day. An uneasy silence followed during which Batak and Englishmen looked accusingly at Indonesians, and Indonesians glared at Batak with undisguised venom. I lost control. Hurling abuse at them, I drove my fist through a flimsy door. This was a most

31 The old *Kepala Perang* of Jou –
    fourteen heads and a killer
    crocodile to his own hand

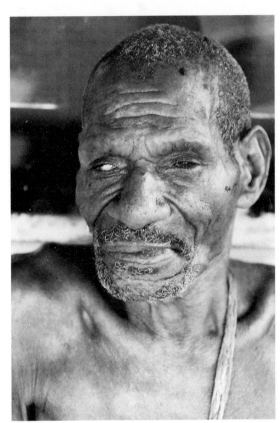

32 Traffic on the Fayit River near
    Basim

33 *Left*, Shand adding to his
own collection of snaps

35 *Opposite above*, waiting
patiently for a deal

36 *Opposite below*, presiding
over a gathering of tribal
ancestors at Buepis

34 *Below*, the young ladies
of Buepis

37 Carrying her head under her arm

effective pantomime of violence; fortunately the culprits fled before seeing the agonised grimace that registered in shock waves across my face. A few moments later they returned, looking sheepish, with the news that the engine would now cost us 9,000 rupiah. Fane instructed them coldly to get it organised; we wanted to depart immediately.

Before leaving, we made a large contribution to the orphanage, and presented our hosts with one of Pak Polici's chickens, which Don had managed to hide the night before. Our young friends lined the bank to see us off, waving and shouting. We waved back, enjoying our shared secret.

★

The journey down the estuary towards the sea suited our mood admirably: it was dull, colourless and oppressive. Piet was silent, distressed by the morning's event. We suspected that he had been bullied by Joseph into attempting the deception.

Nearing the isthmus, the river gradually altered from the usual translucent dark brown to a light muddy colour. I was disillusioned. The Arafura Sea had conjured up images of clear blue water lapping peacefully against dazzling white beaches. Instead, all I could see was mud. Just before we reached the sea, we forked up a narrow tributary, into the lush green jaws of the jungle. Ahead of us was a small armada of canoes. There must have been twenty, each manned by eight or nine large bald-headed ladies. Standing upright, they dipped the paddles in perfect unison, their backsides swaying rhythmically. Some boats carried great loads of green bananas, others bundles of palm fronds, and hardly visible among the loads there were passengers – the men, reclining luxuriously as their women did all the work. What a sensible arrangement! We whizzed up and down, taking photographs, leaving them wobbling in our wake. The women screamed and steered towards the river banks, where they clutched at the overhanging trees.

The supply canoe had passed us and was already moored in the shallows when we arrived at Jou. It was surrounded by a large crowd and dwarfed by the immense longhouse standing behind. The majority of the villagers were dressed in dirty shorts and singlets; only some of the elders were 'undressed' in the more traditional way, bearing themselves with dignity while the others merely looked foolish. It was sad to see this attempt at civilisation.

Jou was a sizeable village, traditionally laid out with rows of rotting shacks dominated by the gleaming white schoolhouse. The school teacher was from Java, and keen to introduce himself. It was a pity we ever laid eyes on this man, for he was without doubt the most garrulous and dull individual I had ever met. He never paused to draw breath, droning on and on in an earnest way about the 'marvellous' job he was doing there and how happy the people of Jou were. Looking round at their deadened expressions, I considered it more than likely he had simply bored them into submission.

He did have one redeeming feature: his wife, a small, curvaceous and deliciously shy lady who was like a breath of fresh air. The schoolhouse was conveniently situated adjacent to their home. Having settled in, we spent most of the day scrutinising her through the zoom lens; there was nothing else to do. When she sidled out to the latrine at the back of the house, we would scramble to 'red alert'. We managed to catch the occasional glimpse of flesh through the tiny gaps in the woodwork, and could clearly hear the sensual rustle of clothing. We knew that she knew we were watching her.

We wandered around the village – or rather stumbled, as the paths consisted of slippery logs which we could never seem to negotiate safely. We teetered like drunks, desperately flailing our arms to maintain balance and inevitably ending up in a heap in a pool of stinking water.

The *Kepala Desa*, or Village Chief, announced his desire to arrange a *pesta* (dance festival) for us. This sounded amusing, and we hung around watching the villagers change from T-shirts and singlets into more traditional costume. The women wriggled into grass skirts, while the men, preening themselves like peacocks, donned feather head-dresses and daubed their chests and faces with white paint. A low noise of drumming reverberated from inside the building, followed by a series of wild cries. The chief, resplendent in his make-up, approached and requested a contribution towards the *pesta*.

'*Bagus*', said Fane. 'How much?'

'*Dua ratus ribu,*' replied the chief.

'Two hundred thousand rupiah!' Fane yelled in astonishment, and still yelling turned to Don and me. 'Do you realise how much that is? Nearly one hundred and eighty dollars! Who the hell does he think we are? Relations of Michael Rockefeller?'

He then informed the chief that we didn't have any money and, abandoning him in a state of some agitation, we returned hurriedly to the schoolhouse in case he decided to include us in some ghastly ritual.

The episode was extraordinary. Here, in one of the most remote parts of the world, they could calmly quote a figure in excess of what an educated person, for example a bank clerk, or even a bank manager, would earn in four months in Jakarta. As usual we placed responsibility with the foreigners who preceded us here. How could they be so stupid?

We were consoled by a visit later on from the village elders. They were a poignant reminder of the past, dressed traditionally, some wearing strange hats made from fur. Piet told us this was the fur of the cus-cus, which my dictionary says is 'a phalanger of the Malay Archipelago', or in other words, 'a small tree-dwelling mammal with pouch'. The most alarming of these splendid gentlemen was the old *Kepala Perang*. His face was seamed with deep scars, one rheumy eye glistening wetly and whitely, and his teeth worn down to jagged yellow stumps. He could barely move without the support of an enormous wooden paddle. He took a shine to Fane and seemed fascinated by the gold ear-ring that glinted enticingly in his left earlobe. The old man's gnarled fingers would reach up from time to time and caress it gently. Proudly he recounted the details of his achievements: how he had taken fourteen heads; the way in which he had slain the crocodile that had terrorised the river, killing over thirty people in one year.

The elders clearly enjoyed our company. Fane and I donned cus-cus hats and pigs'-teeth necklaces, then, grabbing spears, gave an English version of a war-dance. Don delighted them with a magic trick which involved popping a coin into his mouth and then conjuring it from behind one of their ears. This performance was very well received, and he was made to repeat it over and over again.

Back in Jakarta we had devised an idea which we had been saving for just such a moment. The plan was for Don to photograph either myself or Fane trading for some priceless artefact. In place of tobacco or an axehead we would be using the American Express Card. The supporting roles would be played by primitive and unclothed villagers. Our intention was to sell the pictures to American Express to use in their advertising campaign. The captions would read: 'These pictures were taken in headhunting territory by the great Don McCullin. American Express – accepted in over five million establishments worldwide. Don't leave home without it!' It worked well under Don's patient direction, except that the elders seemed more interested in the camera than the card.

Piet discovered that a huge 'sago' festival was to take place in Ochenep some time in the next few days. Members of every village along the Casuarina coast would gather there, making the journey by canoe, and it promised to be a worthwhile spectacle.

CHAPTER TWELVE

Tales of Trade

Fane and I spent an uncomfortable night. We both suffered from a stomach disorder which obliged us to spend most of it perched like canaries on the wooden sill of our window. It was not until the morning that we discovered we had marred the colour combination of the lilies which the school teacher (obviously a man with an eye for perfection) had carefully planted below.

We left Jou at dawn. The entire village gathered on the bank to see us off, some still wearing their tribal accoutrements from the day before. It was as if the opportunity to dress up did not often arise and they were making the most of it. One man stood out from the rest. An enormous pig bone curled through his nose, like an old-fashioned military moustache.

As we slid away down-river, we caught sight of the school teacher's pretty wife standing by herself. She returned our wave, a shy smile flitting across her face.

We soon arrived at the Arafura Sea, the surface of which was smooth as a millpond, although we well knew the potential danger of this coastline. The mud that is continually driven outwards from the river mouths spreads like a brown stain on the surface of the water, while underneath it is stirred into dangerous confusion by the conflicting currents. It finally reaches its shoal mark half a mile out, where the water turns a deep blue. A haphazard line of sticks emerged from the water at acute angles, marking the safe channel; Joseph was unusually alert, his brow puckered in concentration as he steered us through them.

It was a glorious day: out came the sun and the Ambre Solaire. It was a welcome change to enjoy the open space instead of the claustrophobia of the rivers. After only an hour of peaceful sunbathing we headed inland. I scanned the dense blanket of mangrove trees. Joseph seemed to know exactly where to go and competently negotiated a safe passage across the treacherous shallows. At length, I made out an almost imperceptible gap – the mouth of the Forets River, which would lead us to Omandesep.

The river was a hive of activity. Canoes toiled to and fro, propelled by the lusty paddle strokes of broad-beamed women. Causing considerable havoc, we zigzagged between them, stopping to trade, until eventually a traffic-jam built up around us. Drawing alongside one boat, we saw an old man reclining amidships and holding a fine spear with white cockatoo feathers fluttering at the end of the haft. Piet swiftly effected the transaction and we were on our way, leaving the old man the proud owner of a red T-shirt, a coil of fishing line and a couple of sticks of tobacco. I studied my new acquisition. The square hardwood blade was covered with floral designs and the twelve-inch tip was a mass of sharp inverted Vs. Piet told me that the spear was typical of Omandesep, the barbs representing the tails of rayfish. I handed over this lethal weapon to Deo before I stabbed somebody. A little farther on, we passed a canoe filled with a mound of gleaming sea-fish. Fish hooks secured us something far better than tinned sardines for dinner.

Approaching us was a large motorised boat with a gay red and white striped awning. Two individuals with pasty white faces peered out and started to wave, indicating that we should slow down. Instead, we barked a command to Joseph to open up the throttle. As we swept imperiously by, we caught a glimpse of smiles turning to puzzlement and finally to indignation. They were not the only ones to feel annoyed. It had been a rude shock to find *foreigners* in the area: these were the first white people we had seen in weeks, apart from missionaries. We felt our anti-social behaviour was entirely justified. It was more than likely that in violating *our* territory they had already driven the villagers of Omandesep into a positive fever of venality. Apart from that, we simply didn't want anything to do with them.

As soon as we arrived our fears were confirmed. A considerable crowd was milling around on the bank. Grimly, we strode ashore and made for the village. To reach the longhouse one had to cross a muddy creek by balancing on an upturned canoe. Chatting nonchalantly to the villagers, to show we were old Indonesian hands, Fane and I were taken by surprise when the rotten hull disintegrated beneath us and we crashed through. Brushing away the helping hands, we briskly extracted ourselves and continued as if nothing had happened. Mud-stained, and with bruised egos, we arrived at the longhouse.

The villagers filtered in, clutching their possessions protectively to their chests. Fane and I walked around, our eyes raking the goods. In our minds we ruthlessly appraised and discarded, and when something unusual caught our attention we were careful not to extend too much interest. It was the same old game: we could just as well have been in London or New York. When, annoyingly, our tastes would draw us to the same piece, it depended on who had spotted it first.

Don was admiring a small wooden statue of a young Asmatter prepared for war. The owner wanted 50,000 rupiah (forty-five dollars). We thought this an exorbitant price, but Don assured us that it was the perfect memento of our expedition. He called Piet in to initiate the negotiation. The man was forced to halve the price, but was not satisfied. In a state of some excitement, Don dived into the kitbag and spread out an enticing selection of items. After idly fingering them, the man shook his head. Inspired, no doubt, by the Batak's performance a few days before, Don rustled around and produced a brand-new Shetland sweater. The man reached out to take it. Quickly, Piet intervened. Ripping off his stinking jersey he thrust it into the man's hands. It was a classic exhibition of middle-man tactics: Piet now owned a new sweater, and had made something out of nothing.

As we pushed off from the bank, the *Kepala Perang* pulled an object from the bag hanging around his neck. One glance was enough to make Fane leap ashore, with myself in hot pursuit. It was an immense dagger made from the jawbone of a crocodile, the haft decorated with human hair. It was a killer. Fane offered a parang in exchange. He beamed smugly at me. The deal appeared settled. Then for no apparent reason, the chief shook his head, and stuffed his dagger back into the bag. Fane was mortified. An angry exchange flew across the still morning. The crowd, which until this moment had remained quiet, now surged forward menacingly. Piet motioned us to calm down, and some smooth talking defused a nasty situation. We returned to the canoes. Shaken and white-faced, Piet reminded us of what he had said about these people. Of course he was right. Caught up in the spirit of trading we had acted foolishly, endangering the whole crew. We would have to remember that we were not back in the office berating some rapacious dealer: we were deep in headhunting territory and our presence here was delicate, to say the least.

Our next port of call was Basim, a village on the Fayit River, farther down the coast. By the time we reached the sea, the wind had increased, whipping the water into a white frenzy. We crashed through the waves, the prow of the canoe rearing like a startled horse, and soon water was coming through the cracks in the old *Dildo*, requiring emergency bailing. This was exciting stuff, but we were glad to turn in again towards the shore. Surfing in on the rollers, we yelled with pure exhilaration, disturbing a colony of pelicans peacefully sunning themselves on the mud. They took to the air in a turbulent flurry of wings and skimmed away, low over the waves.

The foreigners' canoe was moored at Basim, with an armed guard sitting on the prow. Across his chest hung an empty bandolier and he was clutching what looked like an ancient fowling-piece. He started chatting to Piet and Pak Polici, who had by now arrived looking a little sodden. There was no sign of the pasty-faced occupants who, it appeared, were away talking to the missionary. We decided to push on to Buepis rather than suffer the torture of polite conversation with two total strangers who had so far ruined our day's trading. We were even more anxious to leave when Pak Polici's colleague fished a hand grenade out of his top pocket and started tossing it in the air.

★

I shall always remember Buepis for two things: bosoms and skulls. The minute we arrived the heavens opened, drenching us in an onslaught of ice-cold rain, and a group of young girls ran to the bank to greet us. I imagined that I was Captain Cook arriving in Tahiti. The girls were clad in grass skirts, their skin gleaming in the rain like polished mahogany. Most were on the brink of puberty and the apparition of budding breasts, nipples erect from the cold, was a cheering sight for three weary travellers. Their funny little faces wore wide grins, and they giggled as we dashed clumsily to the shelter of the longhouse. Once inside, Fane and I attached our long lenses with well-practised co-ordination and, surreptitiously poking them through the rotting walls, began snapping away. This was excellent material: some wriggled provocatively, others became shy and covered themselves. One young girl was protected from the rain by an ingenious home-made umbrella made from palm fronds, which covered her head and torso like a giant tortoise-shell.

The rain stopped as suddenly as it had begun. The girls guided us across the slippery meadow to the school hall. It was an enormous room resembling a military barracks. At one end a few chairs stood on a raised dais; these were soon taken by the elders, who had quietly slipped in and were eyeing us in stony silence.

Eager to trade, the villagers started to crowd in, carrying their treasures. Never had I seen such a wealth of bizarre items. The next half-hour resembled the floor at the London Stock Exchange during a gold glut. Trading was brisk and frantic. Fane, the feather freak, scooped up bundles of those G-strings he was so fond of, and also acquired a paddle, known locally as a *dayung*. The blade was incised with scrollwork, the top of the handle carved in the shape of hornbills.

Exhausted by the pressure of high-level negotiations, we had barely sat down when the skulls arrived. Tiny children, pretty girls, old men and women, started to file in, their grandfathers, fathers, mothers and sisters tucked under their arms as nonchalantly as one might carry a rolled-up newspaper. The skulls came in varying sizes and colours. Some had molars still intact, and grinned fiendishly at us. They were placed on the dais in a ghoulish line. Fane and I picked them up one by one. They were smooth and oddly warm. The situation became confused and comically macabre when we began trying to identify their owners. Piet and the rest of the crew were reluctant to have any part of our bizarre transactions. Don, too, was unimpressed. The Batak, however, was not deterred by the aura of evil spirits.

'No, no, *Harimau*,' he exclaimed, 'this' – holding aloft a particularly small and yellowish exhibit – 'is mother of old man *here*, not *that* one!'

Fane and I became hysterical when, at one point, he was juggling with an armful of clacking relations. After we had succeeded in matching most of the skulls with owners, a few still glowered, unclaimed. Could one of these be the missing anthropologist, Michael Rockefeller? Was it the one with the bulging brow? Another sported a fine set of teeth. I wished I was better informed about cranial structure. Finally, I told Deo to ask the villagers, but the mere mention of Rockefeller's name was greeted with laughter.

'He not here, *Harimau*,' Deo said. 'Maybe next village.'

I was particularly attracted to one skull, larger than the others and wonderfully polished. Its greenish patina resembled that which is found only on the rarest of Roman or Egyptian antiquities. The owner was slightly embarrassed to be selling his grandfather, who was firmly wedged between his feet. He kept his eyes glued on the skull, apparently in secret communication with it, as if seeking approval of our offer, but we failed to reach an agreement.

Meanwhile, Pak Polici had discovered from the foreigners' policeman that the sago festival which was to take place in Ochenep had happened the day before. Don was understandably upset, for it would have provided good photographic material. Fane and I were more resigned, for we had experienced these situations countless times. It was a typically flexible pattern of events described by the Indonesians themselves as *jam karet*, or 'rubber time'.

Later, while lying quietly beneath my mosquito net, my eyes were involuntarily drawn to the dais: the skull was still there. The old man had left it to work its spell on me during the night.

CHAPTER THIRTEEN

Pole Position

A stentorian voice woke me. '*Satu, Dua, Tiga*' (one, two, three). Bidding the skull a sleepy good morning as I passed the dais, I slipped outside. In the schoolyard fifty young girls, clad in grass skirts, were being pushed through a strenuous routine of PT. I went to fetch my camera. Don and Fane turned down my invitation to a little lechery in favour of early-morning shots of the river – clearly a far more moody and meaningful experience – but the Batak was predictably keen to join me. Our arrival caused the carefully co-ordinated eurhythmics to dissolve into a confused tangle of limbs as the girls desperately attempted to cover their bare bouncing breasts. When they recovered their composure, they started again, this time with their arms crossed firmly over their chests. Deo and I roared with laughter. They looked like naked little Cossacks. Then the school teacher approached and politely asked us to move, for we were upsetting his pupils.

Back in the school hall, Fane and Don were discussing cloud formation. We started to pack up in readiness for departure. By now we were all pretty disgusting to look at, each of us sporting a heavy growth of beard. Don's was particularly splendid – grey and bristly, resembling the backside of a porcupine. The growth was constantly sticky and matted with bits of old food, but at least it gave our faces some protection from the mosquitoes and other insects that continually harassed us. It was a mystery that they didn't consider them suitable nesting sites. Fane and I spent hours dissuading Don from using his razor, but I was certain that, secretly, he rather liked his new 'wild look'.

The word 'wash' had become alien to Fane and me. I admired Don's tolerance. He was a stickler for cleanliness, and travelling with such companions must have been a disgusting experience. Fane and I felt that, in these circumstances, the dirtier one was, the better. We were convinced that the more filthy and smelly we became, the more likely we were to deter mosquitoes. Our theory seemed to work rather well, for we were rarely bitten, while Don became their favourite food.

Sartorially, too, Fane and I had sunk to a new level of squalor: we were still wearing the clothes in which we started out. In contrast, Don always managed to maintain a certain respectability, perhaps partly due to his diligent change of underwear. Fane and I both noticed that on some mornings a smell of extraordinary sweetness, a smell of spring entirely alien to our surroundings, would permeate the air. We couldn't understand it. Neither of us had taken to wearing scent; had Don? It seemed unlikely. At last, overcome by curiosity, we questioned him. He reluctantly confessed that the smell was coming from his clean undergarments. Before he left England, his girlfriend had washed them lovingly in a fragrant detergent called 'Bounce'. He was ribbed without mercy. Whenever that flowery bouquet perfumed our mornings, Fane and I would break into a lisp and accost him: 'Morning, sweetheart. Mmm, you smell lovely!'

On board the *Dildo*, we swopped places every day to vary the degree of discomfort. At the stern, you could stretch out a little on one of the spare fuel drums. The most undesirable place to be was amidships. There you were destined to nothing but hour after hour of contorted misery. For'ard, you could recline luxuriously on the tarpaulin. This was known as 'pole position', so named because of the immediate access it offered to the shore. Hearing the sound of the approaching engines, the villagers sometimes lined the banks, clutching their treasure in anticipation of trade. The lucky occupant of 'pole position' would be excellently placed to spot the best bargain. Fane and I were very antagonistic in our trading, and this small advantage could be of vital importance. The worst situation of all from this point of view was to be in the stern when Don was amidships. He was far more interested in photography than in trading, and in no hurry to leave the canoe. Unless you were willing to dive overboard, or risk incurring his wrath by trampling on his equipment, you were obliged to wait, seething with impatience, as he carefully assembled his cameras. These were tense moments.

Bakair was a most uncaptivating place which stank of good missionary work. A large red tin church arrogantly dominated everything; an albino sat on its steps, idly picking his nose. The people were clean, polite, and had nothing of interest to trade. We moved on.

At the next village, I was unlucky enough to be trapped in the stern while Fane was in 'pole position'. Even before the canoe had nosed into the bank he had sprung ashore with most untypical agility. He had spotted a superb skull, which he now held aloft, a triumphant grin on his face. Grudgingly, I congratulated him. The skull was unparalleled in its splendour, a true warrior's head. It was the colour of a conker, the eye and nose cavities filled with blood-red seeds. Three glittering fangs protruded from one side of its jaw, and the cranium was crowned with a grand head-dress of cassowary and cockatoo feathers. It radiated power and cost Fane dearly – a parang and two shirts.

I asked Piet to tell the villagers that I too was looking for skulls. Several of them peeled off from the crowd and returned to their dwellings. In a few moments they were back, offering me the grisly remains of their ancestors as a child might present a bouquet to visiting royalty. Most of them were in a sad state of disrepair; the jaw of one was loosely held on by a piece of string, and its owner kept wiggling it up and down like a ventriloquist's dummy, so that it clacked sickeningly. One specimen caught my eye. Compared with Fane's, it seemed ordinary, yet something in the expression intrigued me: it actually seemed to be laughing. Life, I'm sure, had been a big joke, and when the curtain finally came down, he or she had been thoroughly enjoying something. In exchange for an axehead, it was mine. Fane christened our new travelling companions 'the Twins', and they were reverently placed in their new homes – two empty biscuit tins. Piet did not want them in the *Dildo*, so they were entrusted to the Batak in the supply canoe.

We decided to push on to Bajun, a village further down the Casuarina coast. On arrival, we were surprised to find that it was situated on a strip of beach – not one of great beauty, but nevertheless a place where we could at least stretch our legs and walk for a change. In the last ten days, cramped in the canoes, bent double like arthritic old men, we had had no chance to take any exercise.

The sleeping quarters arranged by Piet were not comfortable. The lopsided old shack, built on the beach and isolated from the main part of the village by a row of palm trees, was the home of the *Kepala Perang*, who had retired from headhunting and taken up fishing. Inside, it was dark, hot and stank of fish. The rafters were festooned with nets and various trappings of war that now lay idle and disused, mere ghosts of more exciting days. In one corner, an old man was busy blackening the shell of a drum, holding it above a small fire and then testing its resonance with sharp taps of his fingers. The rafters were so low that we had to erect our nets on all fours, at first helped by the weak sunlight that filtered through the narrow entrance, but soon in darkness as it became blocked by the curious villagers. Sweat poured off me, and the incessant tapping began to drive me mad. I crawled to the entrance and jumped down to the beach where I was joined by Fane. The sea air revived us and we strolled along the shore carefully avoiding the piles of human excrement that lay like molehills on a garden lawn. It was very peaceful. We walked in silence, our only companions the flocks of sandpipers that just kept their distance by running a few feet ahead of us. The beach ended abruptly in a muddy lagoon. We sat down on a piece of driftwood and smoked a cigarette. In front of us, as motionless as herons, stood a few lone fishermen, their bodies half-submerged in the shallow water as they silently watched the play of their nets.

Walking back along the beach, we saw in the distance a white man approaching us. Thinking it was Don, we hurled some friendly abuse, dropped our shorts and, bending down, gave him the old Antipodean salute. The man stopped dead in his tracks. It wasn't Don, but a perfect stranger. Fixing our trousers, we mumbled an embarrassed apology. He did not seem at all offended and introduced himself as Brother Jerry, the resident missionary of Bajun. We mentioned that we were planning to leave from Ewer on 5 September. He had bad news. After days of torrential rain in Agats the airstrip was completely out of action. We were not surprised to hear about the cancellation of the Merpati flight, but it was alarming that not even light aircraft could get in. If it continued to rain, Brother Jerry foresaw the cancellation of all flights for some time.

We rushed back to tell Don. He was freaked out by the idea of being stranded in Agats, as his girlfriend was due to meet him in Bangkok in about a week's time. Piet, who had been watching us with some concern, asked what the matter was. Fane explained. Piet did not consider it to be any sort of a problem. If Ewer was waterlogged, mission aeroplanes could always land at Basim, where the airstrip was founded on sand.

We sat around and discussed the situation, eventually deciding to fly out from Basim on 3 September. It seemed a pity to cut short our expedition, but getting out was the first priority, especially after Fane told us that our cash was running low. Summoning the Batak, we wandered over to visit Brother Jerry and request him to radio Agats to inform them of our change of plan.

The missionary's house was positioned in a lush grove of coconut trees. He was engaged in a little private Bible reading with a young convert called Carl, but seemed pleased all the same to show us around. He agreed to radio Agats the next morning and relay our message. We were disappointed to find he was an abstemious man: no sign of a drink was forthcoming,

38 A traditional mask costume, now banded by the Indonesian government as symbols of headhunting

39 An Asmatter wood carver proudly displays his work

40 Trading in Spear City

41 Fane and Shand conduct enthusiastic bargaining

42 Time to pay up

43 Navigation on a narrow tributary: *left to right*, Fane, Alphonse, Shand; *in the foreground*, Pak Polici, Piet and Joseph; Deo at the helm

44 Heaving the canoe out of the slime

45 Last evening at Agats

so we left. A crowd was waiting at the hut in anticipation of trade. We sifted through their wares but found nothing of interest.

Dinner was jazzed up that night, courtesy of Pak Polici. Spurred by the thought that I might present him with my radio at the end of the trip, he was doing everything possible to win my favour, and tonight produced a chicken. It was my old friend, the randy rooster. It was a little stringy, but didn't taste too bad and, overcome by a sudden surge of generosity, we offered a leg to Don.

Pouring rain, a squadron of mosquitoes and a demented drummer beating a violent night-long tattoo resulted in no sleep. On top of this, we were prevented from leaving Bajun by the low tide: a glistening landscape of mud stretched as far as the eye could see.

Again we visited Brother Jerry. For some reason, the mission in Agats was unable to alter the date of our flight out. At least the rain had stopped there; if the clement weather held, then the airstrip at Ewer would be usable.

The tide rolled gently in. The water was now deep enough to float the canoes. We turned inland and headed up the River Kronkel *en route* for Simsagar. Huge Nipa palms grew along both banks, their long graceful fronds swaying in greeting as we swept by. The large village was a friendly place, and I saw no signs of missionary zeal. We made our way to the longhouse and, to avoid the sun, Fane and I climbed up the outside and sprawled comfortably in the shade of the eaves. Soon a sizeable throng had assembled below. Goods were passed up to us, and we examined each piece. *This* was the way to trade. We felt like rajahs, regally reclining while our people spread below us, servile and silent, honoured to bestow their gifts upon us. Simsagar would be remembered as 'Spear City'. We carefully selected the four finest examples. The tip of one was a jagged mass of human bone barbs.

Don was busy photographing our trading. He had also managed to coax out a group of bare-breasted girls who earlier, on seeing me striding towards them with my camera, had fled into the safety of their dwellings. They now fell willing victims to the Great Man's charm and were giggling as they posed languidly for him.

We moved on to Santambor. On the way, we surprised a group of naked girls who were busily fishing. In vain they attempted to cover themselves with their fishing nets, and ran away shrieking with laughter. The village was filthy and stank of excrement. We were offered two inferior skulls and I was almost bitten by a dog. The *Dildo* became bogged down but, helped by a group of children, up to our waists in mud, we finally pushed it out to sea.

Close by was Japtambor, where we had planned to stop for the night. The people here were aggressive, particularly the school teacher, who demanded a fortune to let us stay in his home. Luckily a young man whose grandfather had died a few days before approached us to say that his house was now empty; we were welcome to stay for a small contribution.

The villagers tried to crowd into the hut and became very agitated when Don cut off their access by drawing up the pole leading to the entrance. Fane could hardly walk. He had been stung by something, and his foot was like a football. Don and I whiled away the remaining daylight hours by watching an energetic game of volleyball, which became rowdy once Joseph decided to join in. Down at the river we watched the women as they collected their water in long bamboo tubes.

Dinner was a meagre affair, for we were running very low on food. Later I produced a bottle of vitamin pills, curiously named 'Up'. Fane explained to the boys that these were powerful aphrodisiacs which turned one into a rampant sex-maniac. They became wildly excited and I promised to leave them behind at the end of the trip. Fane warned them to take only *one* pill; if they took two they would need a new girlfriend as well as a new bed. They talked enthusiastically well into the small hours, the conversation remaining on one track. I heard Joseph boast that he intended taking *three*.

Later, lying underneath my net, I became rather melancholy. I had grown fond of its billowing green shape and my organised little world within. In a few days, we would be back in civilisation and I would remember those first nights on the rivers when, needing to relieve myself, I had lifted up the side only to retreat, wincing with pain, as the mosquitoes descended upon the tip of my unfortunate organ. Now, with practised ingenuity, I simply wrapped it in a piece of loose netting and pissed through the floorboards, laughing silently as I heard the frustrated whine of the insects. I had become a real professional.

CHAPTER FOURTEEN

Skulduggery

On Sundays, in a good mission village, any form of commerce was strictly forbidden until after church. From our hut, we could see the congregation file dutifully to worship, the devout in their Sunday best, others completely naked, most dragging reluctant children. The school teacher began droning out some lengthy sermon, to be replaced at last by clear, bell-like voices bursting into song. By then, some of the elders were sneaking out of the back entrance, keen to start trading. Obviously Mammon was mightier than God around here.

Fane and I finally struck gold. Beautifully carved *dayungs* appeared, bundled together like cornstalks in a wheatsheaf. Reluctantly we rejected them for they were too long to fit into the Cessna aircraft. As I was leaving the hut I noticed, wedged up in the rafters, a serrated harpoon head made from some kind of bone. At first I was tempted to steal it but, remembering this was the Lord's Day, I replaced it with a piece of tobacco, wrapped up in a T-shirt. It seemed a fair exchange.

After a rainy passage, we arrived at Pirien, wet, cold and shivering. We took shelter in the longhouse, where we found the entire village huddled around small fires. They invited us to join them and one old man, concerned by the state of my health, proceeded to give me a vigorous back massage. I presented him with a cigarette before permanent injury was inflicted.

The inhabitants of Pirien were well versed in the ways of salesmanship. Their wares were displayed in a professional manner – rather like viewing day at an auction house – the better pieces lying near the entrances so as to benefit from the light. Fane and I piled up armfuls of goods like greedy men at a buffet. The Batak was in fine form, berating some 'Beach Johnnie' (as he now referred to the Asmatters) for trying to rob him blind for a feathered bag he was admiring.

Fate then dealt us a cruel blow. Even though we had missed the sago festival, we had been looking forward to getting to Ochenep because of its reputation for fine carvings. Now we heard it was deserted. There had been a long-standing dispute with a neighbouring village over the ownership of some sago trees. The inhabitants of Ochenep considered themselves the rightful owners and had left to claim their property. We were advised to stay away from the area.

Disappointed, but not enough to involve ourselves in a headhunting raid, we decided to continue up the coast to Biwar-Laut and stay there for the night. Before leaving, we experienced an interesting example of Indonesian logic. Earlier, the outboard on the *Dildo* had been playing up and the boys, no doubt considering our safety and comfort, wanted to change the engines round. Although we knew it was futile to argue, we suggested that it might be simpler if we travelled in the supply canoe – but no, this was far too complicated, and we watched in resignation as they struggled to complete the laborious task. The change of propulsion required a change of crew: we were now piloted by Alphonse and 'protected' by Pak Polici.

We left the isthmus and had hardly reached blue water when we noticed a boat speeding towards us from the shoreline. I glanced behind. It wasn't the supply canoe, which was to our left, and it certainly wasn't the Austrians: this boat was much larger and had no awning.

Showing no signs of slowing down, it continued to approach. We could make out five figures, three standing in the prow.

'Christ! They're carrying guns!'

One man was shouting angrily, gesticulating to indicate that we were to follow the boat back to the shore. I looked at the others.

'What the fuck's going on?'

Pak Polici was crouched, trembling, under the prow. Piet was ashen white and shaking. He refused to meet my eyes, until my nerve and temper cracked.

'Piet!' I screamed. 'For Christ's sake, who are these people?'

His eyes bulged with fear. 'Polis,' he stammered.

'Police!' exclaimed Don, horrified. 'They look more like a bunch of pirates! That's an M-16 you're looking at! These boys mean business.'

They certainly bore no resemblance to any police we had ever seen. They were dressed in an assortment of guerrilla-type apparel – camouflage jackets, paramilitary fatigues. Their leader, the man who had shouted at us, was all in black, a revolver strapped to his thigh. A blood-red scarf was tied around his head. He looked like a member of the Khmer Rouge.

We flattened ourselves at the bottom of the canoe, squeezing behind the steel boxes for protection against the fusillade that we expected at any moment to blow us out of the water.

The leader screamed at us again. We had no option. Followed by the supply canoe, we made for the shore. Pak Polici, who was still wedged under the prow, was frantically whispering something to me, repeating it over and over again, but the water crashing against the bottom of the canoe drowned his voice. Besides, I was far too frightened to understand what he was trying to say. My mind turned constantly over the events of the past weeks, searching for some clue.

At the mouth of the river there was a small encampment. The police were clearing the village. Doors of the huts were flung open and the terrified villagers forced out and herded into their canoes like cattle, falling over one another in panic. Some of them jumped into the water.

'The bastards,' Don hissed. 'They don't want any witnesses.'

'What do you mean?' I hissed back.

'I've seen it happen before.'

We stumbled ashore, sinking thigh-deep into the mud.

There was silence – only wind and rain. Deo scrambled out of the supply canoe and joined us. He looked more nervous than I had ever seen him.

'Deo!' whispered Fane urgently. 'It will be better if they don't know we speak Indonesian. *Mengerti? Kami tidak bisa bicharra bahasa Indonesia!*' He spelt it out in soft, savage bursts. We had discovered that in these kind of situations, it was always better to play the dumb tourist. Deo seemed to understand, nodding quickly.

As we squelched awkwardly up the bank, I found myself staring at the maker's label on Don's anorak. '100% Nylon. Made in England.' England! I'd have given anything to be in dreary old St James's now. This was just a nightmare. This could not be happening to me.

The leader awaited us. He was shaking, and a muscle twitched below his left eye. The others formed a semi-circle, fingers curled round triggers. One of them fiddled constantly with his safety-catch. Click-click. Click-click.

The leader started shouting.

'For Christ's sake, Deo, what's happening? What's the problem?'

'Yes, yes, Boss. Please, *pelan-pelan*. This man like bomb. Make dangerous for us. I find out.'

The tirade seemed endless. He fixed us with a reptilian stare, his eyes never left our faces. My hands were trembling so badly that I stuffed them into my pockets. I felt the oddly reassuring shape of a camera, but this did not seem an appropriate moment to take a snap. I tried to concentrate and was able to gather a few facts, which Deo then confirmed.

'These men Ochenep police. Angry man Boss.'

We offered to shake hands. The officer ignored us.

'When in Bajun we not see police. *Surat Jalan* not stamped. Now we in big trouble. We not have permission go here.'

We all looked accusingly at Piet and Pak Polici. Fane acted quickly.

'Listen carefully, Deo,' he said slowly. 'Tell the boss we

realise we have made a big mistake and we are very sorry. It is not our fault, we are only tourists. Piet and Pak Polici should have told us in Bajun.'

The officer listened, eyes narrowing, as Deo translated. He stared at us again and then nodded slowly. He swung his attention to Pak Polici and Piet. The other men lowered their guns and walked over to Alphonse and Joseph, who were sitting in the canoes. I glanced at Fane and Don. It looked as though the crisis might have passed.

'What do you think?' I whispered to Don.

'Dunno. I don't trust these guys.'

Suddenly, the officer's voice rose again. We heard the word '*tengkorak*' mentioned several times.

'Shit!' exploded Fane. 'He's talking about skulls. Deo! What the hell's wrong now?'

Looking worried, he explained. The police had received a report that Westerners were trading for skulls at up-river villages. This, he told us, was strictly illegal and punishable by severe prison sentences.

We were appalled. Why had our crew neglected to tell us of this law?

'Now we're for it,' I mumbled.

'You two are for it,' corrected Don. 'I never wanted anything to do with those bloody bones.'

'Look,' Fane cut in. 'We're all in this together. It's the boys' fault again, not ours. We weren't to know. Deo will manage to explain.'

'Cannot,' Deo stated firmly, looking more worried.

'What do you mean, cannot?'

'Piet, Pak Polici very frightened, very stupid. Already tell Boss police no skulls!'

'*What?*' we gasped.

We were now in a terrible dilemma. The police were only carrying out their orders, and through the mouths of our loyal crew we had, albeit inadvertently, lied to them. I now understood only too clearly the reason for Piet's excessive distress and Pak Polici's urgent whispering as we were coming ashore. They must have known all along that trading for skulls was forbidden. The future did not look good. I prayed that we might escape without being searched.

Things looked even grimmer when the officer announced that we must accompany him to their headquarters at Kamor, five hours up-river, where our papers would be processed. This would certainly involve a thorough search of the canoes. The thought of rotting in some jungle jail, our plight unknown to the outside world, flashed through my mind. I felt helpless, trapped. Desperation prompted Deo into making a final inspired effort on our behalf. (The following conversation of course took place in Indonesian.)

'I beg you,' he pleaded, clasping his hands earnestly. 'Please for you to let us go. It is problem of myself and crew, not check with police. Not their fault. They not know. He,' pointing at me, 'very sick, maybe die if not have medicine.'

The officer glared at me. I smiled sickly, and shivered.

'These men not like tourists. They very important. Maybe you get trouble if you make problem.' And, with a flourish, he produced the document from the British Embassy.

The officer snatched it from Deo and held it upside-down.

'This paper,' Deo continued, 'from British Boss in Jakarta. Look!' He pointed to the letterhead.

The officer ran his finger over the seal.

'What is written here?' he demanded.

'It say all in our country make help for my friends. They same royalty, much power. This one, Shand, he married to Foreign Minister.'

In his excitement Deo was becoming rather muddled. I dared not look at Fane and Don. We watched, spellbound. Sweat dripped down my back. Our destiny was entirely in the hands of the Batak and the officer.

He thrust the document back into Deo's hands.

'You!' he snapped, pointing at the three of us, 'Go! You!' turning to Pak Polici – 'come to Kamor. Bring the *Surat Jalan*.

The Batak, exhausted, winked at us victoriously. I realised I had been holding my breath.

We thanked the officer, pumping his hand almost too vigorously. 'Tell him that we'll remember him for his helpfulness,' Fane said to Deo. A glimmer of a smile flitted across the officer's face.

We returned to the canoes, the mud impeding a headlong dash. We were just about to board when a curt order was snapped out.

'*Periksa prahu!*'

Surely this was the end. Two policemen clambered in and started sorting through our possessions. Kitbags were emptied, rucksacks rummaged in and orchids trampled. Feathers and spears flew everywhere. Standing next to Don, I could feel his fury as his camera box was investigated. One of them picked up a biscuit tin. I felt sick. He tried to prise off the lid, which was stuck. He shook it, and then with a grunt, threw it down. They returned empty-handed to the bank and stood watching us as we boarded the canoes.

At that moment, we realised that we had overlooked one important detail. The bloody biscuit tins were still in the supply canoe, which was going to Kamor. It seemed impossible to transfer them without arousing suspicion.

'*Pak Polici!*' I whispered. 'Pass the biscuits!'

Although his command of English was practically non-existent, we dared not risk speaking in Indonesian. Even as I spoke, the tea-party words sounded ridiculous.

He looked at me, puzzled. '*Apa?*'

I tried again, this time pointing surreptitiously at the tins and miming a munching motion. Another blank look – God, was he stupid! The policemen shifted restlessly. Sensing something was wrong, the officer moved towards us. Deo, who was still on the bank making polite conversation, instantly understood our predicament. With typical ingenuity, he whipped out the Embassy document and managed to distract the officer's attention.

In the canoes our game of charades continued. At last, the penny dropped. Pak Polici swallowed his fear and acted with uncharacteristic coolness. He wrapped the tins in my plastic sleeping mat and quickly passed the bundle over to me. I glanced at the bank: nobody had noticed. 'The Twins' were safe, undetected.

We waited while Alphonse tried to start the engine. Nobody spoke. Deo joined us in the *Dildo*. We smiled at the police and waved to Pak Polici and Joseph. For once that cocky grin was wiped off his face. Laboriously, the canoe churned up the narrow channel. The tide was out and we immediately stuck fast in the mud. We got out – we pushed – we moved – we got back in – the engine died. Alphonse clambered out and announced the propeller had fallen off!

'Must go back!' he squeaked in alarm. We all jumped into the water. Nobody was keen on that idea.

'I've got it,' Don shouted triumphantly.

I glanced back at the bank.

'Hurry up! I think I can see them coming.'

Incredibly, the split-pin was still there, wedged into the hole by a blob of mud. Alphonse rammed the propeller back on. The engine fired with the first pull. He slammed it into gear and the canoe shot forward. We reached deep water, and were free.

I remembered something the great Duke of Wellington had said to Thomas Creevey, the diarist, the day after the battle of Waterloo. 'It has been a damned nice thing – the nearest run thing you ever saw in your life.' It seemed an apt description of our own situation, but our troubles were not yet over.

We decided to head straight to Agats, rather than stopping at Biwar-Laut, feeling we would be safer there. It was a foolish choice. Ahead of us stretched some fifty miles of treacherous coastline, most of it to be negotiated in darkness. A solid grey curtain of rain now restricted visibility to thirty yards. Alphonse, peering anxiously ahead like a blind man, was relying totally on his innate sense of direction. Above the sound of the engine I could hear his high-pitched cries as he urged Piet and Deo to bail out faster. The *Dildo* seemed on her last legs, with water pouring through the gaping seams. We had no lights, no paddles, and an engine which was temperamental at the best of times.

I knew that we were in almost exactly the same area, and experiencing the same circumstances, that had led to Michael Rockefeller's tragedy. It was now alarmingly easy to see how that accident could have occurred. I wondered what we would do if the canoe capsized. There wasn't much of a choice. We would either be shark or human fodder. We huddled down in the canoe. I tried to distract myself by concentrating on removing the strips of dead skin from my nose, which soon littered my poncho like confetti. Mercifully, I fell asleep.

I was woken by the howling wind and something banging against my ear. It was Fane's foot. We were being tossed around like puppets as the canoe, engine screaming impotently, was lifted clean out of the water by the oncoming swell, and then slammed down with sickening force into the troughs between each wave. Alphonse had tied himself to the stern and was hanging on to the rudder, fighting to keep us on a straight course. Jagged forks of lightning, accompanied by deafening thunder, split the dark skies and lit up the coastline in a weird phosphorescent glow. We fixed our eyes on the shore. Each time it was illuminated we shouted confidently to each other that Agats must be just around the next point. It never was.

'Let's sing,' I suggested. 'People always sing in times of distress.'

'I don't know any songs, I can't sing, and anyway I'm too wet,' Fane moaned from beneath a heap of plastic.

'I'll get the Batak to sing. He'll cheer us up.'

'Canoe dead ahead,' Don yelled suddenly. 'Jesus, we're going to hit it. Turn the bloody boat!'

We squinted into the darkness and just caught sight of four terrified faces looking up at us from a tiny canoe, as it shot past on our port side. Then it was gone, swallowed up by the sea.

'Shit. That was close! We've got to turn around. We must help them,' Don implored.

'If we try and turn now, we'll be broadside to the sea. We'll be smashed to pieces,' I argued.

'But they'll die.'

'So will we.'

'We've got to have light. Where's the torch?'

'The bulb's broken.'

The journey, for me, was like reliving a nightmare. Unlike the others, I knew from personal experience how utterly helpless one is in these situations, entirely at the mercy of the elements. A few years before, I was hit by the full fury of a hurricane (called 'Bernie') off the island of Guadalcanal, in the Solomon Islands. My boat, the *Camping Loo*, was an eight-ton yacht, considerably more substantial than our present conveyance. The wind had picked it up as if it were a feather and, after spinning it end over end, spat it out on the shore, where it was pulverised into matchwood. Luckily, I had already elected to swim for it, having tied myself to a plastic jerry-can before jumping overboard. I tried not to think about that now.

For two more hours, we had to suffer this storm which had appeared from nowhere, bursting out of the night to wreak its vengeance on us. For the second time in the space of a few hours we were in a highly dangerous situation, except in this case, it seemed, even more so, as there was nothing whatever we could do.

I tried praying, but that didn't seem to work. Come on, I thought to myself, think of something nice, something good. Cut out this horror! Food! That's it. Wonderful English food. Sunday lunches. Roast chicken, Brussels sprouts, bread sauce. Tea at Fortnum's. Watercress sandwiches, thick crumbly biscuits.

'Biscuits,' I yelled. 'We've got one unopened tin left.'

'We're keeping those for an emergency,' Don growled, spitting out sea water as another wave reared over the prow.

'What the fuck do you think this is then?! Fane! See if you can find the tin. It's somewhere in the back.'

'Here. Deo was sitting on it.'

I ripped off the lid. My hand touched something smooth, something feathery. Even above the roar of the wind I could hear the laughter.

'*Ah duh, Ah duh!*' (a kind of Indonesian 'Oh, shit'). '*Harimau* eat skull!'

Order was restored and the right tin found.

'Come on, hurry up, Fane. I'm *starving*! See if you can find me one with cream in the middle.'

'I can't see a bloody thing.'

'Watch out!' Don warned. 'There's a big one coming. Quick Fane, close the lid!'

The canoe nose-dived alarmingly.

'Sorry. Too late,' Fane said, depositing a soggy lump in my lap.

'Christ! They're disgusting,' I complained. 'They taste of nothing. Like cardboard. What I'd really like now is a Chocolate Bath Oliver. That's a real biscuit.'

'Hey, Fane,' Don yelled. 'Chuck over another one. They're not that bad.'

'They remind me of prep school,' Fane choked. 'Sunday nights and evensong.'

'We used to put them down new boys' trousers,' I said.

And so it went on. Clinging to the sides of the bucking boat, our bodies half-submerged in water, we munched away nonchalantly.

★

'Agats! Look! I can see the lights. We've *made* it!' Don shouted, spraying us with soggy crumbs.

We crested another wave. There it was, the lights dancing in the haze of the lashing rain. Never would I have imagined I could be so glad to see it, but at that moment I'd have tangoed with Brother Jim, if he'd asked me. As we gained the shelter of the bay, the storm seemed to subside, grudgingly releasing us from its grip, and we limped to safety.

Later, in the privacy of our room at Manu's house, we slipped the tins containing the Twins under the bed. Considering the day's events, I began to wonder whether Piet and the boys might not be right about the aura of evil spirits which they claim surrounded the skulls.

'Don.'

'Yeah. What is it? I'm trying to get some shut-eye.'

'What's the first thing you're going to do, when you get back?'

'Laraine. And drink a pint of vodka.' He yawned. 'Well, maybe the other way round.'

CHAPTER FIFTEEN

Weather-beaten

The routine of the last weeks had become too deeply ingrained. We were bored and restless.

Piet took us to see a local dealer who spent his time combing coastal and up-river villages for the best examples of local work. Three tumbledown rooms, dark and musty and festooned with cobwebs, revealed a wealth of objects. I was reminded of the first time I crept secretly into the attic at home, when I was a small boy. A watery light filtered through an ivy-covered window, illuminating the most wonderful of hidden treasures. Old leather trunks were stuffed with army uniforms, reeking of mothballs. In one corner, gleaming dully, lay my father's ceremonial sword and, near it, an empty revolver holster, once immaculately polished and now turning green with mould.

Fane and I methodically inspected each room. Behind stacks of shields lay old, dusty carvings. One I particularly admired: three warriors sitting hunched in a canoe. It was a perfect memento.

In the afternoon, Joseph and Pak Polici arrived back from Kamor. Our *Surat Jalan* was now officially chopped and the canoe had been searched. They hinted that money had changed hands but we ignored them.

We wandered over to the mission. At the entrance we met Brother Jim. I noticed that in our absence he had dyed his hair black. Standing in the lengthening shadow of the mission cross, he looked rather more pious than I recalled. Our charter was confirmed for Thursday morning and would be bringing Brother Ed, who had been away on mission business in Jakarta.

I hoped that the late arrival of our aircraft was not due to him: maybe the temptations of the big city had delayed him a couple of days . . . We arranged to return on Wednesday to finalise details.

That evening, Pak Polici informed us that, by direct order from Jakarta, all baggage was now being searched at both Merauke and Ewer. No skulls were to leave the country. However, he had formulated a plan. He volunteered to hold the Twins in his safe-keeping right up to the moment when we boarded the aeroplane and were ready to take off. Then he would rush on to the airstrip, clutching a package and shouting that he had a special farewell present for us, and pass the Twins through the window. He sat back, delighted with the cunning simplicity of his scheme. Fane and I were convinced that he had invented the baggage search story in order to show off his true bravery, as he was determined to possess my radio.

However, the plan did hold some appeal. If by some remote chance an eagle-eyed official should check Pak Polici's package, we would remain innocent. How were we to know the contents of a farewell present? We visualised a pleading Pak Polici under close arrest . . . it seemed a splendid plan, and we congratulated him on his ingenuity.

Although we left Agats early, by the time we reached the open sea the wind was already blowing strongly and the water fairly rough. The old *Dildo* rapidly filled up. Rather than risk another near-calamity, we decided to miss out Biwar-Laut and instead visit Beriten and Owus, which were closer.

We arrived at Beriten. Fane and I were shown some very ordinary objects, nothing to compare with what we had seen in Agats. However, Don discovered a carving which, in its originality, held a certain charm. It was of an old warrior, sitting cross-legged. On his knee perched a hornbill which he was feeding from a small bowl. The owner wanted 20,000 rupiah. I felt it was time to produce my secret weapon. I rummaged around in my rucksack, and with a flourish extracted a pair of very scanty black satin knickers. I had intended to use them myself – for trading purposes, that is – but no opportunity had so far presented itself. As we were so near the end of our trip, it seemed a pity for Don to walk away empty-handed. The man looked surprised (though less so than Don and Fane), but once he ran his fingers through their soft sensuousness, he was lost. The deal was clinched.

We pushed on to Owus, taking with us from Beriten three sturdy villagers. We had been told we might need their help, as Alphonse intended taking a shortcut down a narrow river. It turned out to be little more than a tiny stream that twisted and turned like an angry snake, tunnelling its way under an oppressive canopy of Nipa palms. As we progressed, it became dark and gloomy as a church. Guided by one of the villagers, who perched on the prow, Alphonse was performing incredible feats of skill, steering the great length of the canoe around impossibly tight bends. The water became too shallow and the outboard screamed as the propeller churned in the mud. We clambered out and sank waist-deep into the slime. Slowly we heaved the canoe up the narrow channel.

From time to time, where the vegetation thinned out overhead, we arrived in sun-dappled clearings, disturbing clouds of butterflies that exploded into the air like feathers from a burst pillow. At one point, we heard the incongruous beat of disco music and, squeezing round yet another bend, we met a large canoe. It was packed with people, fish, and sago fronds. Balanced on top of a pile of bananas was a cassette player. Some skilful manoeuvring took place, the sides of the canoes scraping together as we inched past. I noticed Alphonse borrowing a little petrol. As usual, our efficient crew had neglected to check the tank when we left. Finally, we reached deeper water and then joined the wider reaches of the River Bow which would lead us to Owus.

Judging by the size of the village, and by the ornately carved poles supporting the longhouses, Owus was rich and productive, and Fane and I hoped we might finally have discovered somewhere that would offer real treasures. Sadly, we were wrong. The *Kepala Perang* tried to extract 1,000 rupiah to allow Don the honour of taking his photograph. The commercialisation that inevitably accompanies civilisation was nowhere more apparent than here. We wandered around the village: each house was well kept, and sitting in front of them the men worked on carvings, churning them out with the speed of a factory. There was an air of great smugness about these people.

In front of the longhouse they had displayed their handiwork in a most professional way. Everything was modern, soulless, lacking imagination. Quantity, not quality, was all that mattered now. It seemed that the foreigners had been there a few days before spreading money around like confetti. The villagers became most aggressive when they realised that we had no intention of doing the same. They crowded around us angrily and we had to force our way through them in order to reach the safety of the canoes. Once again we were aware of the danger. The transition from the primitive world to the twentieth century had happened far too quickly. The people had not been given the time to adapt, and one could see how easily they might revert to their old ways.

We returned to Agats. The Batak had pressganged some Asmatters into packing up our booty. It was like an assembly line: a paddle would disappear in one end to emerge moments later at the other, neatly wrapped and tied up with brightly coloured plastic string. Deo moved constantly among them, checking and chivvying them to work faster. In a gloomy corner, an old man with one eye sat on the floor carefully stitching new feathers on to the sleeves that fitted over the hafts of our spears. Don was running around like a headless chicken. He had been told by Piet that to 'age' his carving he should bury it in mud for a day, so he had given it to Manu's nephew, who had subsequently disappeared. I told him it was under the shithouse . . .

Later, we assembled at the pontoon for our official photograph. Grim-faced as Victorian explorers, we posed against a backdrop of passing canoes, illuminated by the dying rays of the sun cutting through a sombre sky. Alphonse produced two warm beers. We toasted our crew – excluding Joseph, who had not bothered to turn up.

Finally, we went with Piet to see Brother Jim. In gratitude for his help we presented him with our medical kit. We settled our bills and were told to be on the airstrip at Ewer by nine o'clock next morning.

The crew were waiting at Manu's house, this time including Joseph; it was the first time I had ever known them to be punctual, though it was hardly surprising, for we were about to give them their presents. Clothes, Lilos, flashlights were distributed. Pak Polici, of course, had to wait. I would give him my radio the following day, subject to the successful delivery of the skulls. Of course, the boys had not forgotten the 'Up' pills. We told them to wait until the next day. By the time they realised that they did not work, we would be between crisp white sheets in Jakarta.

Five a.m. found us in pouring rain but high spirits at the pontoon. The canoe loaded and we set off, only to return minutes later: the petrol had been forgotten. Our second attempt to leave was successful, but the engine seemed determined to delay us and progress was slow.

About half-way to Ewer, we were overtaken by the mission boat. Our charter had been cancelled due to bad weather. Dumbfounded, we decided in any case to continue: another day in Agats would have driven us all completely mad.

As soon as we arrived, Fane rushed to the mission, which was on the edge of the airstrip, hoping to contact Brother Jim by radio and verify our position. The rest of us took shelter from the rain in a half-finished shack, and waited. He returned a few minutes later. For some reason, the portly preacher had refused to talk to him direct, but a charming sister called Cornelia had come to his aid. Through her he was able to confirm that our flight was postponed until the next day. Joseph and Pak Polici returned to Agats.

We set up camp in a hut close to the airfield. It boasted an evil-smelling outside latrine and a weighing machine, though our primitive conditions were made more comfortable by the timely arrival of three enterprising ladies from the village, who set up a small *warung* (stall). In no time they were supplying us with hot coffee and coconut biscuits.

Realising that we might be subjected to an official check, we decided to weigh ourselves and all our luggage. We found that in spite of losing a lot of weight, together we were well in excess of the limit. We tried again, this time excluding the great bundle of spears and paddles. It was no good; there was just one solution –to leave the Batak behind. He would have to wait with Piet for one more week until the arrival of the ship service between Merauke and Agats.

With his usual strength of character he took the news well, though I could see he was upset. I told him I would wait in Jakarta as long as possible.

'*Tidak apa-apa* (no problem), *Harimau*,' he replied. 'I see you next year!'

Discussing it later, we agreed that for an Indonesian a week is not a long time to wait . . .

I decided to take a stroll up the airstrip, my companions two sandpipers and a strange yellow hawk. It was exactly 750 yards long. I paced up and down for hours, and in a way this activity preserved my sanity. I was beginning to feel ill; my head throbbed continuously and I was experiencing bouts of giddiness. I wondered what deadly disease I had caught.

Later, we tossed and turned on the hard floorboards. Sleep was impossible. Mosquitoes swarmed up in their thousands through the cracks. Luckily, I had removed the sleeping pills from the medical kit before presenting it to Brother Jim. Guiltily I swallowed a few, wondering if I was addicted, but was reassured when Don and Fane requested some too.

It was still dark when we awoke. Nervously we paced around, waiting for dawn so that we could send Piet to check with the mission on the progress of our flight. Pak Polici arrived from Agats; the Twins were now carefully packed inside an innocuous-looking cardboard box. We hid it in the loo.

Our luggage had now been pared down to basic requirements in order to make room for the Batak. Fane and Don were even prepared to leave behind their heaviest carvings, and Piet was willing to take everything on the boat, sending it to Jakarta as soon as he arrived in Merauke. However, when it came to Deo's turn to have his rucksack emptied, and the contents (mainly paperwork and room-service menus from the Mandarin) were dumped unceremoniously on the floor, he acted like a spoilt child and sat sulking in the corner.

The man arrived to supervise the official weigh-in. We were over the limit, but a couple of cigarettes speedily solved that problem. The Batak was on board, whether or not he deserved to be. Piet came rushing back from the mission. Good news: the aeroplane had left Jayapura and was on its way. Petrol drums were rolled on to the strip; pigs and children were cleared off. We waited . . . and waited . . . Minutes ticked by; half-hours turned into hours. We paced up and down, willing it to arrive. Hearing the sound of an engine, we rushed outside and peered into the sky, listening anxiously. But it was only an outboard on the river. It was now nine forty-five. Something was amiss. At the mission we were told that the aeroplane had yet again been unable to penetrate the dense cloud that massed over the mountain ranges. It was now waiting at Wamena for the weather conditions to improve. Sister Cornelia advised us to check back at noon. Meanwhile she promised she would pray for us.

On the dot of twelve we were back at the mission, crowding round the radio. Through the static we heard the faraway voice of Wamena Control, condemning us to more interminable hours of agony: 'Weather conditions too extreme – pilot returning to Jayapura – will attempt again tomorrow.'

In silence, we slunk back and curled up, each in our own private misery, on the hard floorboards.

*

Six fifty-five a.m. found us again huddled in nervous silence round the radio. We all jumped as it crackled into life. The eerily disembodied voice of Wamena Control announced that our aircraft had departed and that weather conditions were moderate. Unable to bear the suspense, we went outside to wait on the strip. Don had become quite insane. He was practising some weird kind of t'ai chi exercise. Stumbling about in his heavy boots in the mud, he resembled an injured ostrich. An enormous pig which was rooting around in the mud took exception to our presence and we were forced to dive for safety behind an oil drum.

Then a great cheer erupted from the mission. We raced back inside to find a smiling Sister Cornelia. Our pilot had conquered the cloud and would arrive in about an hour.

Impatiently we waited, eyes and ears focused skywards, and in what seemed like no time the little aeroplane had burst through the gloom, bumped down the muddy strip and came to a slewing halt. Out stepped Brother Ed, curiously sunburnt, followed by a short bespectacled gentleman – our intrepid pilot.

We bade a fond farewell to Sister Cornelia and shook hands with Brother Ed; he blessed us for a safe passage. The baggage and most of the booty was squeezed on board. Pak Polici had retrieved the Twins from the loo and with an ingratiating smile whispered that they were safely stowed in the Cessna. Pausing just long enough to see his expectant expression turn to dismay, I slapped the radio into his eager grasp. We said goodbye to the boys; Alphonse squeaked, Joseph just managed a smile, and Piet seemed genuinely sorry to see us go. We spun a coin for the front seat. Fane won. Don and I strapped ourselves into the tiny canvas seats behind him, while in the rear the Batak perched precariously on a mountain of luggage.

As the engine roared into life, the boys rushed over and started banging on the window.

'Obat, obat!' (pills).

I stared impassively at them, prolonging their agony. We started to move. I slid open the window and tossed out the bottle. As we flashed over the airstrip I looked down. No farewell wave. They were fighting over the pills.

We climbed steadily, the bright and broad ribbons of the rivers below gradually shrinking until they became mere streams. I gazed down, realising that I was relieved to be going home.

Epilogue

Don flew straight to Bangkok the next day to meet his girlfriend. Fane and I stayed on in Jakarta for two more days: it gave us a little time to adjust and unwind.

We packed the Twins carefully and sent them parcel post to the office. The thought of being interrogated by a customs officer in London did not appeal to us. On the form, we declared them as 'Indonesian Handicrafts'.

Finally, it was time to bid farewell to the Batak. This was not made any easier by the fact that he was very ill. For the last few days, he had lain in a pool of sweat in our suite, shivering violently with a high fever. The hotel doctor diagnosed malaria, but his illness was partly due to emotion. For the last two years I had appeared, to pluck him from his normal environment and, for a short space of time, exposed him to the kind of life he could usually only dream of – and then, just as suddenly, he was hurled back. There were tears in his eyes when he left, but I wasn't unduly worried: the Batak is one of the greatest survivors I have ever met.

Fane and I flew to Bangkok where we were to stay for a few days with friends. On arrival, we heard reports that an abortive coup to overthrow the government had just taken place. It had lasted for only two hours but, tragically, two reporters were killed. We rushed to the Oriental Hotel, and with relief found our ex-combat photographer relaxing in the unparalleled splendour of the Noël Coward suite. He had slept right through the coup, though sadly he discovered that one of the men killed was Neil Davis, an old friend from Vietnam.

I was beginning to feel extremely odd and without further delay booked myself into a clinic for a full check-up. Apart from suggesting I might benefit from a disinfectant bath, they found nothing wrong, but on my release I began to experience alarming bouts of paralysis that attacked my throat and tongue. I was unable to speak and when I tried it sounded as if I had a cleft palate. I never found out what caused my temporary illness, but remember it as 'Abu's Revenge'.

★

Back in England, we began to run out of unsuspecting audiences to thrill with our tales. Don returned to Somerset, Fane and I put on suits and ties: it was business as usual.

An expert in tribal art from one of London's leading auction houses came to appraise our collection of carvings. Fane and I imagined huge sums. After what seemed a very perfunctory inspection, the expert announced in that supercilious tone that is the trademark of those establishments: 'Charming, absolutely charming! Beautiful quality – but I'm afraid they're relatively modern and therefore not *really* for us . . .' Visions of an evening sale, a hardback catalogue, disintegrated. We listened as he explained that 'really all the great pieces were taken by Michael Rockefeller', when there was a knock at the door.

'Parcel post – delivery for Shand and Fane – sign here please.'

Two square boxes with Indonesian postmarks were deposited in our hands. We ripped them open, and there, nestling among the wads of pink loo paper and grinning fiendishly at us, were the Twins. The expert studied our friends with interest.

'Hmm! Now these are something different – very fine examples. This one,' he said, pointing to Fane's skull, 'is particularly good. I would put an estimate of five hundred to a thousand pounds on it. I have a client who would be interested: he collects only human remains.'

We declined. The Twins meant a great deal to us. We had been through too much to see them end up displayed in some kinky collector's private ossuary.

Later, after he had gone, we sat and admired them; the

memories flooded back. I remembered Joseph's brick-toothed grin, Zacchius's pendulous lip; our first sight of the orang hutan; the vibrations of the *Dildo* and the agony of the tin boxes. I wondered whether Brother Jim had dyed his hair a different colour, and if a certain Asmatter was wearing black satin knickers. I longed to be back there.

As I was idly smoothing the crumpled feathers on the skull's head-dress, a thought struck me: what on earth had happened to my trussed-up feathered friend? Somehow, I knew that he had escaped.

> *If I were a cassowary*
> *On the plains of Timbuctoo,*
> *I would eat a missionary,*
> *Cassock, band, and hymn-book too.*

(Bishop Samuel Wilberforce, 1805–73)

Acknowledgments

First, I would like to thank Harry Fane and Don McCullin. Nobody could wish for two better travelling companions.

To Gita and Sonny Mehta and Abner Stein no acknowledgment can be adequate. Without them this book would certainly never have happened.

My deepest gratitude to my mother, who had to put up with so much.

Both in England and Indonesia so many people, too numerous to mention, lent their support, but I would particularly like to thank the following, who went out of their way to be helpful.

In England – James Barclay; Annette Campos; James Chichester; Anthony Colwell; Marjorie Crodelle; Gwendoline D'Urso; Andrew Fraser; Nickolas Grace; Dr Anthony Hall; Sir Geoffrey and Lady Howe; Nadia Lawrence; Stuart Marshall; Julia Parker; Dr Christopher Powell-Brett; Mary Sackville-West; and Mary Wright.

In Indonesia – Brothers Ed and Jim of the Agats Mission; Mayorpol I. Wayan Diana; F. S. Djodi; H. E. the British Ambassador, Mr Allan Donald; Linda Garland; Kamal Kaul (General Manager, Bali Oberoi Hotel); I. Wayan Ledang; Martin Reed (Resident Manager, Mandarin Hotel, Jakarta); Margaret Rothwell; Mark and Tina Scrase-Dickens; and Sister Cornelia of the Ewer Mission.

A special thank you to Helen and Rolf von Büren in Bangkok, whose hospitality is always legendary, and, most important, to Marie for not allowing a struggling author to wallow in self-pity.

Finally, I would like to thank the people of Indonesia whose spirit, welcome and sense of humour always make this country so attractive to visit.

Bibliography

Barclay, James, *A Stroll Through Borneo*, Hodder and Stoughton, London, 1980

Gardner, Robert and Heider, Karl G., *Gardens of War – Life and Death in the New Guinea Stone Age*, Random House, New York, 1968

Loeb, Edwin M., *Sumatra – Its History and People*, Verlag des Institutes für Völkerkunde der Universität, Vienna, 1935; Oxford University Press, Kuala Lumpur/Singapore, 1972

Mitton, Robert, *The Lost World of Irian Jaya*, Oxford University Press, Melbourne, 1983

Oey, Eric (ed.) and Hoefer, Hans Johannes (director and designer), *Indonesia – for the Sophisticated Traveller*, Insight Guides, APA Productions, Prentice Hall/Harrap/Lansdowne, London, 1985

Schneebaum, Tobias, *Asmat Images*, Asmat Museum of Culture and Progress, 1985

Tenison, Marika Hanbury, *A Slice of Spice – Travels to the Indonesian Islands*, Hutchinson, London, 1974

Wallace, Sir Alfred Russel, *The Malay Archipelago*, Macmillan, London, 1894

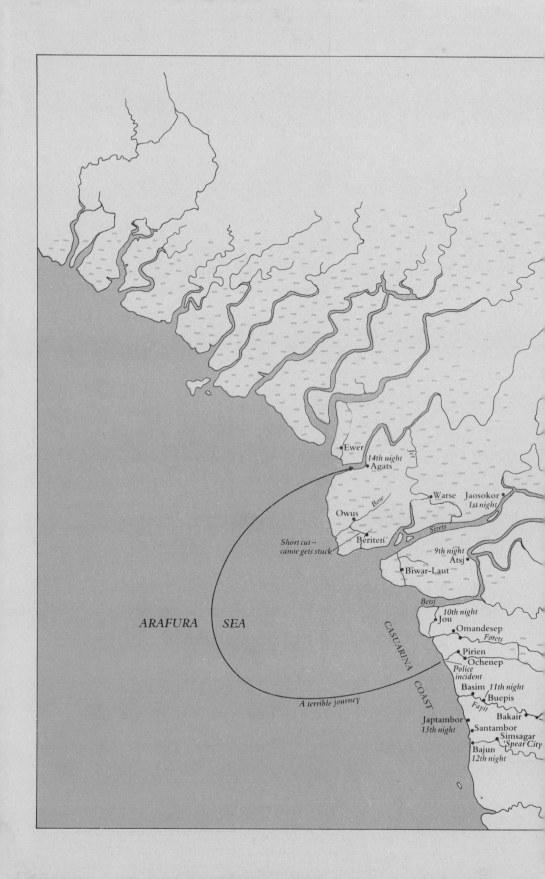

ARAFURA   SEA

Ewer

14th night
Agats

Warse   Jaosokor
1st night

Owus

Short cut –
canoe gets stuck
Beriten

Sirets

9th night
Atsj

Biwar-Laut

Betsj

10th night
Jou
Omandesep
Forets

Pirien
Ochenep
Police
incident

Basim *11th night*
Buepis
Fayit
Bakair

A terrible journey

Japtambor
13th night
Santambor
Simsagar
Spear City
Bajun
12th night

CASUARINA   COAST